MERCER'S MOMENT

Fans celebrate Mercer's win as Duke faithful stand in shock. (Courtesy Mercer University)

MERCER'S MOMENT

Mercer Beats Duke!

DANIEL SHIRLEY

Mercer University Press | Macon, Georgia

40 Years of Publishing Excellence, 1979–2019

MUP/ P588

© 2019 by Mercer University Press

Published by Mercer University Press
1501 Mercer University Drive
Macon, Georgia 31207
All rights reserved

9 8 7 6 5 4 3 2 1

Books published by Mercer University Press are printed on acid-free paper
that meets the requirements of the American National Standard for Information Sciences—
Permanence of Paper for Printed Library Materials.

Printed and bound in the United States.

Book design by Burt&Burt
This book is typeset in ITC Slimbach & Rockwell

ISBN 978-0-88146-717-8
Cataloging-in-Publication Data is available from the Library of Congress

The Bears traveled to Raleigh, North Carolina, for the NCAA tournament. (Courtesy Mercer University)

To Laura, Ben, and Matt
for supporting me every day
and to the Mercer University
players, coaches, and fans
for this exciting ride.

Mercer's athletic mascot, Toby the Bear. (Courtesy Mercer University)

ACKNOWLEDGMENTS

During my many years (more than twenty-five now, wow!) as a sports writer, I've gotten to know many coaches and players well. Easily, Bob Hoffman is one of my favorite coaches ever, and not just for his excitable presence on the sidelines and his terrific postgame interviews. Hoffman is genuine, and the love he has for his players is obvious and comes through in everything he does.

When Doug Pearson pitched the idea for this book to me, I thought it would be the perfect topic to write about. I was around those Mercer University teams enough to know Hoffman well (I got to know him even better later, during my tenure as the sports editor at *The Telegraph*), and I knew the players well enough that I figured they would open up to me. Plus, I was around for most of the excitement and disappointments for those Mercer teams, and when the 2013–14 team finally broke through and reached the NCAA Tournament and beat Duke University, it was a special time to be in Macon.

During this process, the players were tremendous, taking time out of their busy lives to recount stories from their special teams. The seven seniors who are really the focus of this book—Monty Brown, Kevin Canevari, Daniel Coursey, Jake Gollon, Langston Hall, Bud Thomas, and Anthony White—are some of the best young men you will ever come across, and T. J. Hallice, who was a junior on the 2013–14 team, is right there with them.

Jim Cole and his staff with the Mercer Athletics Department have been great, as well, getting me everything I need as far setting up interviews and reaching out to the people I needed to speak to. That help extended to Mercer sports information director Gerrit W. Van Genderen and former Mercer SID Andy Stabell for checking behind me on my facts throughout.

Thanks to Jeremy Timmerman, not only for his wonderful foreword, but for also editing the book, and to my wife, Laura, the best editor I know, for catching my many grammar hiccups and for being my rock.

x

FOREWORD

Jeremy Timmerman

Mercer basketball, and the Mercer campus as a whole, has changed. Consider that fifteen years ago, I had already been accepted to Mercer University and had no idea that the Bears had a Division I program. At that time, the Bears were finishing up play in Porter Gym, which held something like 500 people and sat on an impossibly small patch of land not even big enough to play intramural sports on.

When I arrived on campus in 2004, the first full school year that the 3,500-seat Hawkins Arena—then simply known as the University Center—was in use, the athletics department still had that small-time feel. You could show up, basically, whenever you wanted for basketball games and sit wherever you wanted, unless it was homecoming.

And really, that's unfortunate. There were a lot of players on those teams who deserve to be remembered more than they are. Damitrius Coleman led the whole country in assists in 2004–05, the same year James Odoms got the Bears on *SportsCenter* with an absurd game-ending sequence. I missed that game—a rarity during my time at Mercer—because I was frustrated by how the team had been playing, and, boy, did I regret it.

After them came players such as Calvin Henry and James Florence. J-Flo seemingly could score at will in the A-Sun Conference. The 2007–08 team went across the country and beat highly regarded freshman O.J. Mayo and Southern California, yet no one seems to remember that because of how the rest of that year went. The Bears finished 11–19 after that season-opening win at USC, were eighth in

Left, Mercer lost the 2013 A-Sun Tournament championship game at home to Florida Gulf Coast. Right, Florida Gulf Coast's players celebrate in the closing minutes of the 2013 A-Sun Tournament championship game at Mercer. (Courtesy A-Sun Conference)

the A-Sun, and lost eight conference games by ten points or fewer. They lost five A-Sun games by six points or fewer.

Then came head coach Bob Hoffman, whose introductory news conference was one of the last events I covered for the student newspaper, *The Cluster*. After I moved on, I heard from friends how he and his staff would ride around campus trying to recruit students to come to the games. Interest in the team spiked, and the Bears started winning not just the random marquee games, but also the conference games that really matter in a one-bid conference like the A-Sun.

The Bears had one more letdown for me to watch in person, the 2013 A-Sun championship game that saw Florida Gulf Coast win the conference's bid and go on a run in the big tournament. The next year, I watched from an Applebee's in Columbus, Georgia, (following the USC Aiken Pacers on a run to the Division II Final Four as a reporter) as my Bears did what we had been dreaming of and won the A-Sun. Then I watched from home as they shocked the world and allowed all of us to say, "We beat Duke."

The story of that 2013–14 team is the stuff sports movies are made of: a new coach takes over a sputtering program and eventually brings in an almost-too-special-to-be-true class from all over the country. That

Florida Gulf Coast head coach Andy Enfield celebrates after his team won the 2013 A-Sun Tournament championship game at Mercer. (Courtesy A-Sun Conference)

team draws one of the top three or four college basketball programs in the world and then goes on to beat it, basically in the favorite's backyard. That well-constructed team becomes the nation's darling and helps push an entire university's momentum to the next level. That would be a good movie, and it would be 100 percent true.

Daniel Shirley is the right man to tell that story. He has been a boss, mentor, and friend to me for about twelve years now, and no one knows sports in Macon and Middle Georgia quite like he does. He's gone big-time at *The Athletic* now, but his perspective on what Mercer's basketball win meant to the campus and the area is a valuable one.

I enjoyed this book, and even as an original Mercer Maniac, I learned some things about the program. Please enjoy it, and be sure to stop by Mercer sometime to take in a game. It's worth it!

MERCER'S MOMENT

Mercer Beats Duke!

Mercer's players charge the floor in celebration of their win over Duke. (John Domoney)

FAVORITE MOMENT

What the Bears' players, head coach, fans, and administrators remember most fondly from that moment and that season.

It was a moment no one involved with Mercer University—the school or the basketball program—likely will ever forget. For the coaching staff, the players, and Mercer's administrators and fans, beating Duke obviously was *the* moment.

But there were so many other moments and memories leading up to that day—March 21, 2014—when the Bears' basketball team placed the word "Mercer" into the national consciousness.

Everyone involved will remember that day as Mercer turned the NCAA Tournament on its ear with a 78–71 win. In a tournament known for upsets, this one wasn't to be upstaged. It was a No. 14 seed beating a No. 3 seed, so that made it memorable.

The fact that it was *that* No. 3 seed, Duke, pushed it over the edge, and Mercer's players, coaches, and fans danced right over that edge in celebration.

But it wasn't the *only* moment or memory that mattered for head coach Bob Hoffman, his team, or the Mercer fans.

"I think that our camaraderie and the feelings that we had for each other's successes, whether it be an individual play that someone made on the court all the way down the line to someone getting an individual award or our team winning and everyone having their own contributions and such, the joy in those things and what we felt for each other was special," said Jake Gollon, one of seven seniors on the 2013–14 Mercer team. Jake continued,

> We still feel it. When Daniel Coursey got engaged to his girlfriend or Monty Brown got married and had his son, the group texts were still flowing. They're full of joy and full of humor, and there is a tremendous amount of love there that will always be there and make us special. It sure wasn't basketball talent.
>
> It's the combination of the structure at the top with the coaching staff and the administration and setting the tone for that or at least promoting it. No coach can get his players to love each other. Most coaches can't get their players to love them. But you have to have that door open and promoting it for there even to be a chance, and Coach Hoffman and the staff did a really good job with that. On the flip side, we've got a pretty rare group as players who were open to being like that. We had several guys who were deeply and emotionally invested in the game who simultaneously understood your success in the game can only go as far as the team. We were fortunate in a sense that our coach promoted that and was open about it, and we also had a group of guys who just so happened to understand what *team* meant and who were going to do whatever it took to be good.

That determination had been building for some time with the Mercer program. The Bears had come close to winning the A-Sun title the year before but lost the tournament championship game on their home court to Florida Gulf Coast. And then the Bears had to sit and watch as the rival Eagles went on a run to the NCAA Tournament's Sweet 16, thinking that should have been them.

The year before that, Mercer lost in the semifinals to that same Florida Gulf Coast program when it looked like Mercer could be headed toward a showdown with Belmont in the championship game. So there had been disappointments that led to the season of joy in 2013–14.

On March 9, 2014, Mercer finally got over the hump—and got some revenge to go along with it—with a win over, yes, Florida Gulf Coast on the road for the A-Sun title and a trip to the NCAA Tournament.

"My favorite memory of that group of guys was how determined they were to get that opportunity," Hoffman said. He continued:

Left: Mercer seniors Langston Hall (standing) and Kevin Canevari celebrate after the Bears won the 2014 A-Sun Tournament championship game. Right, Mercer head coach Bob Hoffman cuts down the nets after the Bears won the 2014 A-Sun Tournament championship game. (Brian Tietz)

Mercer fans celebrate during the closing minutes of the team's win at Florida Gulf Coast in the 2014 A-Sun Tournament championship game. (Brian Tietz)

Mercer's Moment: Mercer Beats Duke!

When they came up short the two years before, in the midst of that, how they pushed themselves to work even harder, and they were going to find a way to make it happen. And then when you push forward, and we get to the end of the year, and we tie for the league, but we have to go on the road for the championship game, just to see how they work through that.

Really, we could have lost the semifinal game if it weren't for heroics of T. J. Hallice, who was not used much all the time, but he made some big plays in the overtime for us to win. Probably just the amount of intensity that they put forward collectively to achieve a goal and find a way to make it happen and weren't going to let anything get in the way of accomplishing that together, those things are all special to remember.

That togetherness is seen to this day with the seven seniors, the seven special players who led that team on and off the court. They're still close: Gollon, the player who lasted six years in the program;

Mercer's seven seniors led the Bears to the 2014 A-Sun Tournament championship and the automatic NCAA Tournament berth. (Brian Tietz)

Langston Hall, the ultimate do-everything point guard and leader; Bud Thomas, a talented guard who could shoot from deep and defend on the other end of the court; Daniel Coursey, the 6-foot-10 center who controlled the paint along with Monty Brown, who came off the bench with more defense and rebounding with his 6-11 frame; Anthony White, the junior-college transfer who had to find his way with the program; and Kevin Canevari, who danced his way into Mercer fans' hearts after the program's biggest-ever win.

To this day, those seniors have a group chat going. They share, they talk, they make fun of each other (Canevari said Coursey takes the brunt of the punishment), and they remain close. They most likely always will. "Definitely we accomplished so much, but the one thing that stands out is just how close we were and still are," Thomas said.

> Even to this day, we have the group text and a group chat, and we stay in touch almost every single day, all of us. It's a situation where you're basically living with your teammates, and you're eating every meal with them. It's a unique time in your lives in college, and for us to all click the way we did is special. We played hard, and we played for each other, and I think that's a huge part of why we were so successful. That's something I've learned to appreciate because I know it's not always like that.

The seniors grew close through their careers and their disappointments. They say they were driven by the loss to Florida Gulf Coast on their home court in the A-Sun Tournament title game in their junior seasons. Watching the Eagles celebrate and cut down the nets drove the Bears that summer.

After all, those seniors only had one more chance to get to the Big Dance—the NCAA Tournament.

They had won a postseason tournament before, as sophomores, when they made a dramatic run to the CollegeInsider.com Tournament (CIT) title and played in the National Invitation Tournament (NIT) the next year, including a win at Tennessee. Still, while those tournaments are nice rewards for good seasons, they aren't the NCAA Tournament, and the players wanted their chance to play in the NCAA Tournament.

"What stands out is, we had our senior class, and most of us came into the program together, but we didn't have the kind of year we wanted [as juniors]," Brown said. Further, Brown stated,

> We came together as a group with a team full of young guys. We hit it hard that spring, we only took a week off, and we came back to work that spring, and we worked hard, we had guys there for voluntary workouts. The year before we had a really good spring, a productive fall and that year culminated with the CIT championship, which was a lot of fun. It wasn't the NCAA or the NIT, but for a young team trying to build some chemistry, it was a good turning point for us as a program to get over that hump. To go from a losing season to get to the postseason and to go win a postseason tournament changed things for the program and the school. That sophomore year was a tough one, but it was a turning point in that we came together said, "Look guys, we've got to play together, and we've got to play for one another. We've got to buy into the system," and we all did.

Mercer's players had plenty to be excited about after winning the 2014 A-Sun Tournament championship game. (Brian Tietz)

Indeed, they did, and the win over Duke is the moment most people will point to. But a couple of the players said the win over Florida Gulf Coast that led to the Duke game is *the* memory for them.

"My favorite moment was actually beating Florida Gulf Coast and getting over that hump because they beat us my sophomore year, and then my junior year they beat us again. It was like, 'Man, we have to get past these guys,'" Hall said. "It was special to go down there and beat them and have all our fans down there to celebrate. It was amazing, and words can't even express how that felt, and to know that we had come so far from our freshman year to our senior, it was just unbelievable."

Even in that win, the Bears had to show their mettle, which they had done for years. They dominated the first half against the rival Eagles and looked like they would cruise to the NCAA Tournament.

But Florida Gulf Coast used a big second-half run in front of its passionate fans to make things interesting. Still, the Bears never lost control and celebrated on the Eagles' floor after watching the Eagles celebrate on their floor the season before.

"Winning at Gulf Coast, because that had been our goal all year, to win the conference championship, is what I will always remember," Canevari said. "The year before that they had cut down our nets, and that left a bitter taste, and it was a huge moment for all of us and definitely a goal for all of us to bounce back from that and cut down their nets."

Even Hoffman's wife, Kelli, points to that win as *the* one. Yes, beating Duke was unforgettable, but finally taking down Florida Gulf Coast was . . . well, it was memorable:

> Nothing matches the emotion of beating Duke, obviously, but when I think of that team and everything they had been through together, the rivalry with Gulf Coast was probably one of the major, I'd say the major rivalry, we had, and when we beat them at Gulf Coast, that was amazing. And just the celebration afterwards. Of course, we had gone through a couple of those celebrations in the locker room when somebody else was celebrating on our home floor, and, of course, Gulf Coast being one of them. To have that opportunity for this group of young men on Gulf Coast's floor was really special.

And then came Duke. Some folks were surprised when they saw Mercer's name pop up on the television screen opposite the national powerhouse during the NCAA Tournament selection show.

Coach Hoffman wasn't one of them.

"The afternoon of the selection show, early in that afternoon, I ran into Bob Hoffman, and I said, 'What do you think?' He said, 'I think we get Duke. I've been looking at it, and I think we get Duke,'" Mercer president Bill Underwood said. "I said, 'What do you think about that?' He said, 'Great matchup for us.' He said, 'If I could pick somebody, that's who I'd pick.' And what do you know, hours later, we get Duke, and then we go beat them. I will never forget Bob telling me that day we were going to play Duke."

But it wasn't just the game, the forty minutes of thrilling upset action. Yes, that was something Mercer fans always will remember, but there was more.

There were the seven buses filled with students and faculty and staff members that made their way to Raleigh, North Carolina, to cheer on the Bears against the Blue Devils. Then it was those students and faculty and staff members flooding into the PNC Arena as a "sea of orange" and showing off the Mercer spirit.

Mercer's director of Campus Life, Carrie Ingoldsby, and her then-assistant, Cindy Strowbridge, put together that trip and got to enjoy everything that went along with it.

"The excitement, the energy in our crowd. Cindy and I really jumped on board and got involved. It was really exciting to be a Mercer staff person and to get to enjoy that with all the students and enjoy watching them all go nuts and watching Coach Hoffman and the players on the floor," Ingoldsby said. "That part was just so exciting. The walk from the buses to the arena was really cool, really great. We all felt very proud to be a Mercerian. Even though I was a staff person, as opposed to a student or an alumna, it was a real moment of pride to be affiliated with Mercer and to be one of the people who was the point person to planning the trip and getting all those students there."

And those students helped put Mercer on the map that day.

"Hands down, this group walking across the campus and the parking lot and chanting, 'We are MU,' it was loud, and everyone was watching us," Mercer vice president and dean of students Doug Pearson said. "The energy was high. Everyone hates Duke, and they were coming up to us wishing us luck. There was a sign, a person came up to us, and it read, 'Mercer fan since March 16' because they didn't like Duke. Everybody was coming up to us and talking, and it was so supportive and wanting us to beat Duke. When we walked across that parking lot and into the arena, it felt like a home game."

The Bears then played like they belonged, even against *that team*. Duke has won five national titles (it had four at the time), while Mercer had never won a single NCAA Tournament game. Still, it was hard to tell which team was the ACC and national power and which team was playing in the NCAA Tournament for just the third time.

Duke led by one point at the half, but Mercer hung close and scored twenty of the game's final twenty-eight points to pull away.

There were big moments (White's layup after a long inbounds pass from Thomas for a six-point lead with forty-four seconds to play stands out) and some small (individual realizations in the closing moments that it was over as Gollon hit four free throws in the final eleven seconds to seal the win).

"I would say the whole thing, but I guess that's not specific enough," White said with a laugh. He continued,

> One of my own personal memories is when I hit the 3 to tie the game with two minutes left. But the whole team, when it started to hit us, after Jake got fouled, and he was at the free-throw line. The way the camera was set up, you could see me and Lang, and we were like, "We did it" and gave each other a hug, and that was probably my favorite part.
>
> My second favorite was having my family there, and then walking into the arena after the game, and we got a standing ovation, and that was special. I guess it was because it was Duke and everybody hated them, so we got a standing ovation. We were walking up into the stands afterward, and all you could see was Mercer orange and North Carolina blue, and the North Carolina fans were like, "If you guys want to come to campus, you're welcome any time. We'll pay for anything. Come on." We couldn't because we had another game, of course, but it was a good time.

There were plenty of good times with this group, and those were not confined to that March day.

"Not one particular moment but the whole experience of it all," Coursey said of his moment to remember:

> I know people want to remember the Duke game as our one defining moment, and it was, but I remember the little things, like when we were roommates and the pregame stuff in the locker room and all the small funny things. That's mainly what I remember when I think back on it.

I do remember the Duke game and everything that led up to it, but when I think back on those teams, I remember the little things and the goofy things of us being together.

Oh, and there was plenty of goofy that day. Canevari showed off this team's fun-loving side and took the sports world by storm with his version of the Nae-Nae dance craze in a postgame dance circle with his teammates as the large sea of orange-clad Mercer fans celebrated with them.

Rick Cameron, Mercer's senior assistant vice president for marketing communications, has been the "voice of the Bears" since the 2006–07 season after originally doing radio play-by-play in the late 1970s and 1980s, and he has seen plenty of Mercer wins during his time. He saw plenty of silly, playful moments with this group.

None will hit him like this one, and he was almost right in the middle of it.

"Obviously, . . . Kevin with the dancing, that was unbelievable," Cameron said of the memorable day.

Kevin was always dancing in the pregame. When they would warm up on the floor, Kevin would lay down on the floor, and they would reach down and grab him and pick him up to dance. So Kevin was always dancing and doing things like that. When that game is over, we're all just pinching ourselves, and reality had not set in. And, of course, that massive group of students was sitting right behind me, and I could hear them the whole time. I could sense Jake and Kevin coming over, and I thought they were just going to come over, "Yeah, we did it" and celebrate with the fans.

Then, all of the sudden, Kevin raised one arm. Then he raised two, and the rest of them started backing up, and I'm still live on the postgame, so I'm trying to keep my composure with what I'm saying. I'm thinking, "What the heck is Kevin doing?" I've never heard of the Nae-Nae in my life; I didn't know what was going on. So Kevin starts, and I had that feeling of all the other players being around him. Then, it's like when you go on an elevator, and the more people get in, and you feel claustrophobic, and there are cameras all over and around me. I could sense that Kevin was

Kevin Canevari became a national sensation with his version of the Nae-Nae after Mercer's win. (John Domoney)

stealing the show. Then what he did, going to ESPN in Bristol [CT] and all that, Duke and Kevin are just going to go hand-in-hand.

Bill Underwood said it best that Bud Thomas said that Kevin Canevari would one day do something stupid and become famous for it. Bill tells that story all the time, and that's exactly what Kevin did. It may have seemed stupid at the time, but it got him national attention and got him on ESPN.

That attention took hold after the win and the dancing, but it had been building for years as the Bears worked toward their big moment.

Langston Hall had 11 points and five assists against Duke. (John Domoney)

2

BUILDING THE BEARS

*A look at the Bears' program before the magical
2013–14 season and what Mercer went through to turn
into a national darling with its upset win over Duke.*

Beating Duke certainly wasn't easy, but getting to that point proved more difficult than the Bears could have expected. That journey, however, made the win in Raleigh even sweeter and more memorable for the team and its fans.

The win over Florida Gulf Coast to earn the long-awaited NCAA Tournament trip.

The win over Duke.

And then the dancing and celebrations.

None of that would have happened without the Bears working their way through the highs and lows of the seasons leading up to the 2013–14 campaign.

Bob Hoffman took over Mercer's basketball program before the 2008–09 season, replacing Mark Slonaker as the Bears' head coach. The first season was solid and saw progress with a 17–15 finish, but then the Bears had consecutive losing seasons (finishing 16–17 in 2009–10 and 15–18 in 2010–11) as they worked their way through the transition from one coaching staff to another.

The 2009–10 and 2010–11 seasons were the first two of four straight in which the A-Sun Tournament was played at Mercer, meaning the Bears had to watch other teams celebrate on their home floor after winning the conference title. In the 2009–10 conference tournament, the Bears recovered from an injury-filled regular season to reach the title game only to lose 72–66 to East Tennessee State as the program got a small taste of championship play.

Jake Gollon was there from the start of Hoffman's tenure; he had actually signed with the Bears before Hoffman took over and ended up with the program for six seasons because of several injuries, getting a special exemption from the NCAA for the sixth season.

Hoffman's third season featured a freshman class that included Monty Brown, Kevin Canevari, Daniel Coursey, Langston Hall, and Bud Thomas, with Hall cracking the starting lineup right away.

"I watched the first two years in the conference tournament, one on the road and one at home," Gollon said.

> I remember thinking to myself, "I'm two years into school. I'm 1,000 miles away from home. I've got four years left to get to the NCAA Tournament, and we have at least one or two, if not more, chances of having the conference tournament on our home court. We're going to win this thing." I always had this feeling that the president and the AD put this money up for us to have it on our home court, and we can't blow this. We all know the advantage that home court gives you. So to see the scenario building where we're one of the best teams in the conference, and we have the opportunities at home, and to not follow through on that was always really—I don't want to say depressing—but it was deeply aggravating. It was something that we knew we could do. We were good enough. It was just difficult to comprehend that we were so close to doing something so great, and we just weren't able to do it.
>
> So, going into that senior year, it was a do-or-die year for a lot of guys. Obviously, I think we would have been fine, we're an intelligent group of guys, but had we not won, I don't know what our mindset would have been. Had we not won the conference tournament, had we not gone to the NCAA Tournament with a chip on our shoulder, I don't know what would have happened. We felt so due for that if we didn't get it, it's almost that something could have gone wrong for each of us. It just happened that that's the way it played out. If you want something bad enough for long enough eventually it will happen. If you keep knocking on the door, eventually you'll get there.

Known for his passion on the sideline, Bob Hoffman has helped change the face of Mercer athletics. (Brian Tietz)

Eventually the Bears did get there, but it was still a couple of seasons away, and the 2011–12 season was a big step in making that happen.

That season, the Bears finished 27-11, including 15-3 at home, and they were 13-5 in conference play. The regular season included a 65–59 road win over Georgia Tech, but once again, the Bears lost in the conference tournament at home, dropping a 62–58 decision to Florida Gulf Coast in the semifinals. Mercer had won the teams' two regular-season meetings and appeared to be headed for an appearance in the conference title game before the loss to the Eagles.

But the Bears responded by beating Tennessee State (68–60), Georgia State (64–59), Old Dominion (79–73), Fairfield (64–59), and Utah State (70–67) to win the College Insider.com Tournament championship.

"We all took different paths during our freshman season, and it was a huge adjustment for all of us," Thomas said. "In our sophomore year, we started getting minutes together and playing together and learning each other and what we wanted to do and where we needed

Mercer's Moment: Mercer Beats Duke!

to be on the court. That CIT win was huge for us, because we were all sophomores trying to figure out what we were doing, and that was a huge confidence boost for us."

It was a confidence boost, for sure, and one heck of a ride. Rick Cameron was right there for the entire trip.

Those final three games of the CIT were played on the road as the Bears capped an impressive run. After losing as a No. 2 seed in the A-Sun Tournament to Florida Gulf Coast, Mercer showed its resolve and bounced back nicely from that disappointment.

"Starting that CIT run, they beat Tennessee State; they weren't that fired up about that, but they won. Then they beat Georgia State, and it's like, 'We might as well win the thing,'" Cameron said. He continued:

> Then they send us to Richmond to play Old Dominion, and we played well. Then after the game, it gets to be midnight, 12:30, and we're standing out in the parking lot of the hotel, and we don't know where we're going next. That's the way that tournament works. We're all just standing there waiting and waiting, "Where are we going?" We finally find out we're going to Fairfield, so we have to load a bus to go to Connecticut. Coach Hoffman rents us a rock star bus, one of those with the sleepers in the back, and we all load up on that. We get there, and the main arena that they play in was being used for hockey, so we played in their old arena. To me, that was an advantage, and we win that thing.
>
> So then we're thinking, "We've got the highest RPI, we're going back home, and we're going to play the championship game at Hawkins Arena." The next day, we find out we're going to Utah State, and I get an email from Bobby McDuffie, the violinist, and he says, "Rick, I just want you to know what you're going into," and it's the Utah State kids with their "I believe" cheer. It was unbelievable, and I started telling Hoffman what we're going into, and we could see then why they were hosting with all that support.

Once the Bears got to Utah State, they got an up-close look at the atmosphere and what to expect and, indeed, why Utah State was given the right to host that game. Cameron said it's the loudest arena he has ever heard during his time working Bears games.

"Their sports information director started explaining the setup in the postgame for the losing coach, just plain as day, he said, 'When the game is over, the losing coach will go here and here,'" Cameron said. "And I'm thinking, 'Oh, okay, let's go.' The doors open, and it sounded like a rodeo with the fans running down to the floor. When they started the 'I believe,' cheer, it was unbelievable."

That continued throughout the game, and Cameron pointed to a second-half run made by Utah State as an example.

"I'm looking at the radio gear to make sure we were still going out over the air because it was so loud, I couldn't hear a darn thing. It's just deafening, and I'm just watching the needles to make sure we're on the air," he said.

> But our guys responded to that kind of adversity well, and they were able to pull it out. Winning that thing was a really big deal, and none of us gave them enough credit for what they accomplished. But what it did, it set the stage for what these guys were able to accomplish. The average fan might think, "We just up and beat Duke." And we did, but it wasn't a flash in the pan. You can see for those two years of how we got there.

But again, the reward was still more than a year away, even with another tremendous season in 2012–13. That season, the Bears finished 24–12, including wins over Florida State (61–56) and Alabama (66–59) on the road. They were 14–4 in the conference, winning the A-Sun regular-season title outright for the first time, and they were dominant at home, meaning they had plenty of confidence and momentum entering the conference tournament, which also was played at Mercer.

But Florida Gulf Coast again stood in the way and upset Mercer 88–75 to hand the Bears their only home loss of the season. The Eagles then won two games in the NCAA Tournament, taking the nation by storm with a run to the Sweet 16, and won an ESPY that summer for "Best Upset."

"That junior year was tough because we had such high expectations, and we thought we'd get it done, but then to see Gulf Coast win it and see them go through the NCAA Tournament was hard," Thomas said. "Watching the ESPYs and seeing them going up on stage and

Bob Hoffman and his players celebrate near the end of the team's win over Duke. (John Domoney)

get all the love was hard because we thought that should be us. But all those things were huge in building our camaraderie and how we played together for sure. Our senior year, we were on a mission, and no one was going to stand in our way of getting where we wanted to get and that was winning the A-Sun and getting to the tournament."

The Bears' 2012–13 season, however, wasn't over with the loss to Florida Gulf Coast, as Mercer advanced to the NIT by winning the A-Sun regular-season title. The Bears bounced back from the disappointing loss to Florida Gulf Coast to beat Tennessee (75–67) in the first round of the NIT before losing to BYU (90–71).

Still, the thoughts of the Eagles and their successes lingered throughout the summer for the Bears and their leaders.

As Hall remembered,

We thought that was our year; for sure that was our year to take it. But then losing to Gulf Coast, we knew they were a good team, but losing to them and watching them and what they did in the tournament, it was like, "Man, that could have been us." That drove us the whole summer and the whole year to get back there, and we were motivated to get it done.

We talked about it when it was happening and when Gulf Coast was beating teams in the tournament, like, "Did you see they beat someone else? Did you see what they're doing? Ugh." But we didn't really have to talk about it after the season started. Everybody just realized it was time to go, and we knew what it was going to take to get it done.

That determination stands out in Hoffman's mind, and he takes pride that his players have displayed that kind of grit throughout the years:

> It manifested itself in a lot of ways, differently. I remember Jake Gollon and me having some pointed communication and tough times going at each other to some level—probably not like some people would think—because I wanted it for them so bad that there was probably some negativity from me. I wasn't being as positive all the time as I needed to be, and he was trying to keep me on track with that. And toward the end of that year, the conference season, and we had had some tough things to deal with. Each one of those guys, they would all likely have something different that made them go harder. But the general consensus was that they weren't going to be denied of their chance to get to the NCAA Tournament after they had failed and come up short a couple of times. As we know all throughout history, you can look at any point in history, and we can see that everybody who ends up accomplishing something great, they usually fail first and learn how to fail and how to overcome failure to become successful in anything. Those guys definitely did that.

There were tough losses, certainly, that motivated this team and drove it forward for its special season. And there were big wins that proved Mercer had the necessary mettle once it got on college basketball's biggest stage.

"For me personally, it was when we lost to East Tennessee State [in 2009–10], and we should have gone that year," Hoffman said, recalling how the team progressed after the loss:

> But moving forward with this team specifically, in the postseason we had been really good. We won the CIT and did amazing things that people said we couldn't do. We won at Utah State, where we weren't supposed to win and didn't have a chance,

right? And these guys had never experienced that, which was huge for them, and then the next year we won at Tennessee in the NIT after being disappointed by losing in the conference tournament again. That took a lot of toughness, mental toughness, to bounce back and prove you're that good. I think that set us up for what those guys chose to do and what they chose to be about for the next year.

So the Bears had a taste of wins over big-name teams, and they had experienced postseason success. Both of those would play a huge part for this program once it got its shot at college basketball's biggest stage.

HOFFMAN'S WINS OVER POWER CONFERENCE PROGRAMS BEFORE 2014 NCAA TOURNAMENT

Mercer 72 - Alabama 69 *(November 16, 2008, Tuscaloosa)*
Mercer 78 - Auburn 74 *(November 19, 2008, in Auburn)*
Mercer 65 - Georgia Tech 59 *(December 22, 2011, in Atlanta)*
Mercer 61 - Florida State 56 *(December 2, 2012, in Tallahassee)*
Mercer 66 - Alabama 59 *(December 22, 2012, in Tuscaloosa)*
Mercer 75 - Tennessee 67 *(March 20, 2013, in Knoxville)*
Mercer 77 - Seton Hall 74 *(November 16, 2013, in Macon)*
Mercer 79 - Ole Miss 76 *(December 22, 2013, in Oxford)*

"Our postseason experience and success, I think it was huge," Hoffman said. As he recalled,

> I said before the game, "We haven't beaten Duke before, but we haven't played them." But we had beaten people that had played Duke, the Florida States and Georgia Techs and other people that play Duke all the time. That was the whole premise of what I said to the guys before the game and what we believed in. They had done enough, but they needed to remember those things and why they should believe and how they had done those things. The inner core of the leadership for that team was tight, and they pushed each other to work really, really hard, and they pushed all of us all the time. That's why they were so successful.

3

THAT SPECIAL SEASON

*Breaking down Mercer's magical season that ended
with an A-Sun Tournament championship and a spot in the
NCAA Tournament: how the team finally got over the hump,
after some close calls, to earn a spot in March Madness.*

The 2013–14 Bears entered the season with plenty of built-up aggression after missing out on their chance to reach the NCAA Tournament the season before (and a couple of seasons before that, when they also thought they would make it).

But they also had plenty of confidence. For the seven seniors—Brown, Canevari, Coursey, Gollon, Hall, Thomas, and White—the 2013–14 season marked their final chance to get the job done, and they were ready.

"Shoot, game one, just to be honest," Canevari said when asked when the Bears knew they had something special that season. He continued:

> We had a lot of seniors, and that was our goal from our junior year and really our sophomore year. But as we got older, it seemed like it was more and more likely—we were No. 1 in preseason polls and everything. But really, day one, we knew we had the potential. In sports, there are so many outlying factors. You can have an off night. There can be bad calls, so many things can happen, that to actually get it done is something we're so thankful for.

Once we won the CIT, we started to develop a special competitive chemistry. We already had the off-court stuff, and we were all close friends, but after that, we really started developing as a team. When we got to junior year and that loss [to Florida Gulf Coast the year before], Travis Smith and Chris Smith graduated, and it was their last time, and we weren't able to get it done for them, it really motivated us not only because we wanted to win a championship but we wanted to do it for those guys who didn't get to experience it.

The chance to do that started with plenty of hard work during the summer as the Bears took a mission trip with Athletes in Action to Lithuania and Latvia.

"It was a great trip, and I remember the guys playing good in those games, but more importantly, just how together they were and how excited they were to get started," Hoffman said. As he recalled,

> We got smashed by the Latvian national team, but that trip wasn't really about that. By the beginning of that season, they were really, really good, and we were just praying we could keep everybody healthy.
>
> I'm sure they [talked about the Florida Gulf Coast loss], but we didn't ever talk about it as a coaching staff. The players were awesome. They were just amazing in how they led by example and kept everybody pushing; it was just great.

The foreign trip was significant for the Bears, but it was a bit of a struggle for White, who joined the team the season before as a junior college transfer and was still trying to find his exact role in the rotation entering his senior season.

"I struggled, and Coach Hoffman took me out of the starting lineup, and it was my fault; I had to get better," White said. He continued,

> That's when I kind of earned my starting spot back. Just being in the starting role and understanding the other guys had been together, it was just another point of where I had to get in where I fit in. It was a testament to the other players and the coaches that I had a learning curve, and those other guys helped me get settled in.

But from the very start of the season, we just clicked, and it started working, and it worked the whole season.

After a season-opening loss at Texas (76–73), the Bears were strong throughout the season. They finished with a 27–9 record with a 17–1 record at home, including a 77–74 win in double-overtime over Seton Hall. The road schedule featured a thrilling 79–76 win over Mississippi in late December as Hall came through in the clutch with a 3-pointer with two seconds left and Canevari showed off his dancing skills after the win.

"When Langston hit the game-winning 3 against Ole Miss, that really propelled us," Coursey said. Further,

We thought we were good, and we believed we had a chance to be really good. But that really was the icing on the cake and gave us some momentum into, "Hey, we are pretty good. We've got good chemistry. We've got a great coaching staff. We've got great fans and a great city behind us," and the rest of the season kind of showed that. We had a lot of confidence from that game going into the conference season.

Mercer led most of that game only to have Ole Miss fight back and tie the score on a wild Marshall Henderson 3-pointer with thirteen seconds to play. But the Bears had Hall, and when they needed a play made in the clutch, he typically came through.

"Yeah, it's an amazing memory. I still have the video on my phone, and I still can't believe it happened," Hall said, recalling the moment:

It was crazy because we were up three, and then Marshall Henderson hit a crazy 3 over Ant, who played great defense on the play, and it was like, "Are you serious? We did all this work and that's going to happen?" We were winning the whole game, and he hits this crazy 3. Then Coursey was coming to set a ball screen, and I think Coach Hoffman was trying to call a timeout, but he just ended up letting us play, and I went behind my back and just shot it. As soon as it left my hand, I actually knew it was good. I don't know how, but I thought, "That's going in for sure." That was a big win for us.

Mercer's players celebrate after the Bears won the 2014 A-Sun Tournament championship game. (Brian Tietz)

Hall's game-winning answer set off a postgame dance-party celebration that was a precursor of things to come. And, as Coursey said, it definitely helped spark the Bears to their special season.

Mercer finished 14–4 in conference play, splitting the regular-season title with Florida Gulf Coast. The conference tournament format had changed before that season, with the higher-seeded team hosting each game, and Florida Gulf Coast had the tiebreaker over Mercer despite the two teams splitting their regular-season meetings.

That meant the Eagles would host the championship game this time around if the two teams got that far. They did, but first Mercer had to survive a test against USC Upstate in the tournament semifinals. Torrey Craig, one of the best players in A-Sun history, and who currently plays in the NBA, led that USC Upstate team. But the Bears managed to pull out a win against this formidable team with a little help from junior forward T. J. Hallice. With the game tied in the second overtime, Hallice made two baskets to give Mercer a four-point lead as it pulled out a 78–75 win and earn another rematch with Florida Gulf Coast.

"I for sure remember that game. It was definitely a big game for us," Hallice said about the win over USC Upstate. "A lot of people think

I did something spectacular the last two minutes, but I was just doing my job. My whole career was just about rebounding and defense and doing whatever I could do energy-wise. It just so happened that it was my time to do my job, and it was just at a critical point in that game.

"That's what our team was about, just doing our jobs."

So it was on to Fort Myers, Florida, and the Bears' third meeting of the season with the Eagles.

Mercer had beaten Florida Gulf Coast 68–55 in Macon in January but lost the second regular-season meeting 75–61 in Fort Myers in February.

The night before the showdown, Hoffman took his coaching staff out for dinner to reflect on the season and look ahead at the big hurdle to come.

"We talked about just how proud I was of them and everything we had been able to accomplish. We were staying right by a Ruth's Chris [Steak House], which was kind of fun. Just so everybody knows, that wasn't turned in on any expense report. That was paid for by the head coach," Hoffman said with a big smile.

> That was a fun night, just for us thinking about it and dreaming about what could happen, talking about what we needed to do for our guys. We had already made the game plan, but we were talking more about the excitement of the moment and preparing for that and what we expected the next day. We were also praying that none of the Gulf Coast fans got my phone number because other times we had been there, they would call me in the middle of the night, waking me up. The fans were nuts. My name didn't appear anywhere on any reservation from that time forward, and we stayed somewhere different from before.
>
> That was an amazing moment. Knowing the satisfaction of getting back to that moment with the team as a coaching staff because you just don't know. You never know if you will get back to that point. Just knowing that we were back to that point and getting that chance and seeing what our guys could accomplish was special."

All the hard work and preparation—and even the paranoid attitude about the hotel and the coach's phone number—appeared to pay off with a huge first half. The Bears came out flying and led 33–17 at the half, meaning they were just twenty minutes away from the conference title and their destiny: a long-awaited trip to the NCAA Tournament.

The Eagles, led by point guard Brett Comer and talented stars Bernard Thompson and Chase Fieler, fought back and made the Bears work for it. Mercer, however, held on for the 68–60 win, setting off a celebration with the Bears' fans who made the trip south for the game.

"It would have been special and meaningful for us to win it at Mercer, but for us to go down there with a chip on our shoulder and win it and watch them have to walk off their court was very satisfying for us," Thomas said. "At that time, it was the biggest win of our lives, every one of us, and we thought that it couldn't get any better than that. But there was no way we'd realize what was about to happen."

Finally, this group of young athletes accomplished what it had been driving for all those years together. It was special, and it meant that these players and coaches would get to take that next step, the one they had worked so hard for.

"That's where the five seniors as starters and a couple of other seniors coming off the bench, we celebrated the Gulf Coast win, and we accomplished our goal, and that deserved some celebrating," Thomas said. "But at the same time, we knew that for the seven of us it was our last go-around, and we knew we did what we wanted, and all season, we thought, 'Let's focus and get this back together' because we weren't done yet."

As usual, the Bears were led by those seniors in that memorable game. Hall and White both scored fifteen points, while Coursey had thirteen, and Gollon had twelve. But the Bears were more than just the seniors, as other players stepped up when needed, just like Hallice did against USC Upstate. Junior forward Darious Moten had a key sequence midway through the second half with a basket and a made free throw after Florida Gulf Coast had cut Mercer's lead to three points.

White then hit a jumper, and Mercer's lead was back to eight points as the Bears retook control with a recovery that showed off Mercer's preparation and the tremendous work done by Hoffman's coaching staff.

"Comer would call a play, and we would have our own play for it for whatever kind of action it was," White said of the pregame work the Bears did to prepare for the Eagles.

> We were at the free-throw line, someone was shooting free throws, and Comer looked at us and looked at me and was like, "Why do y'all know every single one of our plays?" I said, "Man, that's just preparation." They came back and made it close, and [assistant coach Doug Esleeck] had told me in the pregame warm-ups, "They're going to hand off to Fieler, and he is going to dribble this way and spin back right in front of you." Well, they called the play, and Coach E barked out the same signal from shootaround, and what did they do? Fieler got the ball and spun right back to me, and I was there waiting for him and got a steal. Darious got an "and-one," and that was huge. That kind of took the wind out of them.

The Eagles did pull to within three points again with less than four minutes to play, but Hall hit a basket, Coursey made two free throws, and then Hall added a free throw.

Mercer's lead was again eight points with forty-one seconds to play, and its leaders knew they were on the brink of finally reaching their goal.

Then came the celebration that was six years in the making.

As Hoffman remembered,

> There was elation, satisfaction, everything all rolled into one after all the work to get to that point and all the guys who had come before who helped us get to that point and to that moment in the six years I'd been here. It does take all those different staffs and all those different guys, the players helping to recruit other players and winning games nobody thinks you're supposed to win before they got here and setting the tone for that group. All that culmination at the end knowing what had happened, it made you just want to sit down and cry because you know what they had accomplished and how special it was and knowing you were going to get to experience something as a head coach and something that program hadn't accomplished in a long time.

Hoffman had been to the NCAA Tournament as an assistant coach at Oklahoma as an at-large team, but at-large berths aren't really there for the A-Sun. No, that tournament championship is about the only way the A-Sun is going to have a team get in, and the Bears knew that.

"At Oklahoma, when we went both times, we didn't win our way there by winning the postseason or the conference tournament," Hoffman said. He continued,

> We were given an at-large berth, so all along you knew you were going, but when you're in a one-bid league, it doesn't matter what you've done to that point.
>
> It's all out the door if you don't get it done on a certain night. You can have one bad shooting night or one kid twist an ankle, and all of the sudden, it's over. All those years of leading up to that could have been gone, so we were fortunate in that, too, and the guys were able to get it done.

The Bears were fortunate that they didn't have any injuries that could have derailed them or many off nights in key situations. But they also had the right mindset, a winning, unselfish mindset that has been showcased time and time again during Hoffman's tenure as the head coach.

"That game in Fort Myers, I think, was the defining moment for that team," Underwood said. He continued,

> That team, better than any team I've seen, just had the right chemistry. Those guys were incredibly unselfish. They knew each other. They played well together. There was nobody on that team whose first priority wasn't the team being successful. That's just a rare thing, even at this level. A lot of times guys are thinking, "I've gotta get my points. I'm going to try to get on in the NBA, or I'm going to try to get on in Europe, and if I don't score, I won't be able to do that." There just wasn't anybody on that team that had that mental outlook, and that paid off for that team with that win.

Ike Nwamu (10) sprints for two. (Courtesy Mercer University)

2013–14 MERCER ROSTER

01 Phillip Leonard - *sophomore guard from Tulsa, Oklahoma*
02 Matt Panaggio - *freshman guard from Daytona Beach, Florida*
03 Kevin Canevari - *senior guard from Charlotte, North Carolina*
05 Bud Thomas - *senior forward from Highlands Ranch, Colorado*
10 Ike Nwamu - *sophomore guard from Greensboro, North Carolina*
11 D. J. Brooks - *freshman guard from Simpsonville, South Carolina*
12 John Mosser - *freshman guard from Cary, North Carolina*
14 T. J. Hallice - *junior forward from Weddington, North Carolina*
15 Anthony White - *senior guard from Indianapolis, Indiana*
20 Jakob Gollon - *senior forward from Stevens Point, Wisconsin*
21 Langston Hall - *senior guard from Atlanta, Georgia*
22 Darious Moten - *junior forward from Bowdon, Georgia*
25 Lawrence Brown - *sophomore guard from Kansas City, Missouri*
32 James Bento - *freshman forward from Houston, Texas*
34 Jibri Bryan - *sophomore guard from Savannah, Georgia*
45 Monty Brown - *senior center from Liberty Mounds, Oklahoma*
52 Daniel Coursey - *senior center from Savannah, Georgia*

2013–14 SCHEDULE (27–9, 14–4 A-SUN)

November 08   Texas, L 76–73
November 13   Reinhardt, **W 95–53**
November 16   Seton Hall, **W 77–74** (2 OT)
November 18   Evansville, L 89–76
November 20   Johnson & Wales, **W 109–56**
November 23   Yale, **W 81–54**
November 26   Ohio, L 76–67
November 29   Valparaiso, **W 117–108** (3 OT)

December 02   Oklahoma, L 96–82
December 07   Denver, **W 64–63** (OT)
December 16   Alcorn State, **W 70–44**
December 22   Mississippi, **W 79–76**
December 27   St. Andrews, **W 98–56**
December 30* Jacksonville, **W 86–49**

January 01*   North Florida, L 89–83
January 04*   USC Upstate, **W 62–60** (OT)
January 06*   East Tennessee State, **W 73–63**
January 10*   Kennesaw State, **W 83–46**
January 16*   Northern Kentucky, **W 74–58**
January 18*   Lipscomb, **W 87–66**
January 23*   Florida Gulf Coast, **W 68–55**
January 25*   Stetson, **W 87–49**
January 31*   East Tennessee State, **W 90–77**

February 02* USC Upstate, L 80–61
February 07* Kennesaw State, **W 75–68**
February 14* Lipscomb, **W 79–48**
February 15* Northern Kentucky, **W 89–67**
February 21* Florida Gulf Coast, L 75–61
February 23* Stetson, **W 73–52**
February 27* North Florida, L 79–76 (OT)

March 01*	Jacksonville, **W 69–55**
March 04^	Jacksonville, **W 85–64**
March 06^	USC Upstate, **W 78–75** (2 OT)
March 09^	Florida Gulf Coast, **W 68–60**
March 21°	Duke, **W 78–71**
March 23°	Tennessee, L 83–63

*A-Sun regular-season   ^A-Sun Tournament   °NCAA Tournament

2013–14 A-SUN SEASON AWARDS

Player of the year - *Langston Hall*   31
Defensive player of the year - *Daniel Coursey*
Coach of the year - *Bob Hoffman*
Scholar-Athlete of the year - *Jakob Gollon*
Tournament MVP - *Langston Hall*
All-Conference First Team - *Langston Hall*
All-Conference All-Academic Team - *Jakob Gollon*

Mercer was going to wear these jerseys for the game against Duke before head coach Bob Hoffman came up with alternative plan. (Courtesy Bob Hoffman)

4

SELECTION SUNDAY

*What that day was like, seeing Mercer's name revealed in
the NCAA Tournament and realizing the Bears would be facing Duke,
one of the nation's true college basketball powerhouse programs.*

The celebration from the win over Florida Gulf Coast was something to remember, and it continued throughout the next week on the Mercer campus as the team and its fans had a week to revel in that while waiting for the NCAA Tournament's selection show.

The players certainly enjoyed the celebration about what they had accomplished and what they had been through to get there.

"There was such a rivalry with Gulf Coast that was aggressive, almost, and wasn't like any of our other games. We fully expected to win the A-Sun our junior season year, but for them to win on our court, that hurt, really hurt," Coursey said. "So, the next year when we beat them there, it was almost twice as sweet. Honestly, I would have rather beat them our senior year than our junior year because they thought they had it, and it was just a much sweeter win, I felt like."

The Bears had played in a lot of big games, a lot of memorable games, and they were preparing for their biggest yet.

"Absolutely, even my junior year, I remember that A-Sun Tournament was huge," Coursey said. He continued:

> I remember the three games were awesome, even though we lost to Gulf Coast. Our senior year, we barely beat USC Upstate, and that game was huge. That's when T. J. had his huge putback

with an offensive rebound and a putback, and we were barely able to win that game. It's weird now, thinking back on it, and which games I remember compared to what other people remember. I remember that USC Upstate game more than I remember probably the Duke game almost. Personally, I was so invested in that game and the rivalries that had formed, and it just culminated in that.

When we all come back together, we all talk about how big of a game that USC Upstate game was, and we barely won that game. No one really talks about that game but us players. When we all get together, we tell T. J., "That was literally your shining moment," that five- or ten-minute period where he was incredibly clutch and really showed up and did the things we needed him to do to win the game. We don't even get to play Gulf Coast and win the A-Sun Tournament and get to go to the NCAA Tournament to play Duke if it's not for the USC Upstate win.

But the Bears did get to do those things, so they had some more work to do even with the celebrations going on around them.

The A-Sun Tournament was played a week earlier than most others, so the Bears knew they were in the NCAA Tournament while other teams were fighting their way through their conference tournaments that week. That gave the team some time to unwind and get ready for what was next, even though the players and coaches had no idea what that was.

Coursey recalled,

Coach Hoffman gave us a few days off to go home and recollect. We all came back, and it was all business. We were all on the same page. There was no joking around or goofing around. When we were going through warm-ups or going through scout-team work, we were all focused, and everybody was paying attention. It was because, "Okay, we always thought we were in the big leagues, and now that we have a chance to play against a big-league team, we need to show up." Everybody needed to be focused and get ready to play. And we did that.

First things first, Mercer had to find out who the team would be playing, and the players and coaches did so in front of a huge crowd

The crowd awaits the announcement of the Bears' opponent in the NCAA Tournament. (Roger Indenden)

in their home arena. Hoffman was clear on whom he thought his team would play.

"Coach Hoffman had been saying all week that we were going to play Duke in Raleigh, and we were all like, 'No we're not. We're going to play this team or that team,'" Hall said. "But he called it from the jump, and when it happened, we were all thinking, 'How did you know that?' But he called it."

Hoffman told his team right before the announcement he thought the opponent would be Duke or Virginia. The two teams were playing in the ACC Tournament championship game, and Hoffman was sure Mercer would face the loser.

Virginia won that game 72–63 and earned a No. 1 seed in the East Regional. Duke was seeded third in the Midwest Regional, while Mercer was seeded fourteenth.

When "Mercer" popped up on the screen to face off with Duke, there was a huge celebration at the Bears' arena, and there was a buzz on the Mercer campus in the days following that announcement.

"The meeting right before that, we were talking, and I told them we were going to play Duke. I really did. I thought we were either going to play Virginia or Duke, whoever lost that game," Hoffman said. "The ACC Tournament championship game back then was right before the selection show, so I felt like whoever lost was going to be

Mercer fans at Hawkins Arena erupt when it was revealed the Bears would play Duke. (Roger Indenden)

a three seed or a four seed, and we would be a thirteen or fourteen; that's what I thought. So I wasn't surprised. I just thought, 'Are you serious? I just told the guys that we would play Duke, and now we're going to play Duke?'"

The players were excited for their opportunity. After all, it was *Duke*. The other No. 3 seeds in that year's tournament were Syracuse, Creighton, and Iowa State. Any of those would have been terrific opponents for the Bears to play.

But this was *Duke*.

As Thomas recalled,

> For us to get Duke, you think Duke, UCLA, and North Carolina, those are the schools you think of when you think about college basketball. So for us to get that draw, we couldn't be happier. And we had the mindset that we were going to go into the game and compete. I wouldn't say we all expected to win, but we all knew we had a chance, and we were going to give it everything we had and play one of the best basketball programs in history. That was good motivation for us.

The Bears knew what was ahead of them, but they also knew they had defeated many power conference teams leading up to that game. During Hoffman's tenure, the Bears had defeated Alabama (twice), Auburn, Georgia Tech, Florida State, Mississippi, Seton Hall, and Tennessee.

So, even though it was *Duke,* the Bears were battle-tested and ready for the challenge.

"I told our guys I felt like it was a good match for us because they weren't real big," Hoffman said. "They weren't like a lot of power conference teams, at least that year. They had great players. They had guys who were drafted. But they weren't like the longest, biggest dudes. In fact, we were bigger than they were, and we thought that would help us."

Yes, Duke had future NBA players in Jabari Parker, Rodney Hood, and Quinn Cook, among other talented players, but the Bears had experience, smarts, and size. Coursey anchored everything from the middle at 6-10, but Gollon and Thomas were both 6-6, and Hall was 6-4, with White rounding out the starting five at 6-2.

That's quality size for a mid-major program, while the bench featured Brown (6-11), Hallice (6-9), Ike Nwamu (an athletic specimen at 6-5) and Moten (also a terrific athlete at 6-6).

"We knew what it took to go up against those kinds of athletes. We all had good basketball intelligence and high basketball IQ, and we had decent athleticism for a mid-major team," Thomas said. He continued,

> But we realized it was going to take us playing a smarter game than the Dukes and some of those programs that just land unbelievable athletes, and we knew what we were facing against Jabari Parker and those guys. We had to use our experience and our cohesiveness against their athleticism, and we all realized that.
>
> At the same time, having Coursey, who is 6-10, that's different from a lot of mid-major teams, and we did have some athletes. Some of those mid-major teams face the big teams, and the athletes are just too much in the end. But we had good athletes. We had Ike off the bench and Langston is 6-4 and a good athlete and Darious; we had some serious athletes who could help guys like me. That was huge for us. People see that size and think about post defense. But it was all the way out to the guards who could play good defense, and if they happened to beat us, we could funnel it into

Coursey, and you're not going to get an easy layup over him. It's a big trickle-down effect that those guys had, and if Coursey got into foul trouble, we brought in another 6-11 guy in Monty. We had bodies to throw at those guys, and that happened to be one of the years that Duke was smaller than usual. I think we were the bigger team, and I think that definitely played a factor.

So Mercer would face the team Hoffman said it would play, and the Bears went to work. They watched film that night, practiced Sunday and Monday, and then headed to Raleigh on Tuesday for their Friday afternoon game.

"It was weird because it was our first time, obviously, playing in the tournament, and a lot of the bigger schools had played on huge stages. We had already beaten high-major teams before, but it's different in the tournament," Canevari said. He continued,

> Going into that, we had to control our emotions and not just get caught up in, "We're a fourteen seed and they're a three, and it's Duke, and they have one of the greatest coaches of all time," and everything that went along with all that. So there was definitely a little bit of a different feel with the atmosphere, and the media coverage was crazy. But it was pretty consistent with how we had prepared for games, and we were ready.

The Bears had a good week of preparation before the announcement that they would play Duke, and they had strong workouts after that. But there was a little drama and adversity about what Mercer would actually wear during the game on basketball's biggest stage.

All season, Mercer had worn white uniforms with white numbers, black uniforms with black numbers, or orange uniforms with orange numbers. After the win over Florida Gulf Coast in the A-Sun Tournament, however, Hoffman was told his team couldn't wear those in the NCAA Tournament. As he recalled,

> They wanted the contrasting numbers for TV and the officials, so when I found that out, I didn't know what the heck we were going to do. We had the whole week, so we call Adidas, and Adidas is part of the deal, too, because they helped us with those

jerseys. So, they were going to send us a stock uniform, which they did. We get the stock uniform, and we take it over to Team Sports [a local Macon store], and they were going to make it as nice as possible. And when they got done, I brought it and showed it to the guys, and they were just sick. It was just heavy, and it looked like a junior high school or high school team; I mean it was awful. So we go through that process, and I didn't know what we were going to do because I didn't want them to feel embarrassed about what they were wearing, and Adidas had no other answers. So I was lying in bed on Thursday night before the selection show, and it just came to me because a long time ago, I worked at Keller Sporting Goods in Oklahoma City, and we used to do these press-on numbers all the time on jerseys and practice jerseys. And I thought, "I wonder if we can cut out numbers that would press on and stay on long enough for a game on there." So, the next morning, I went over to Team Sports and asked them if it would work, and they said it might. I believe we got it done Monday before we left Tuesday. They got them cut out and got the right size and pressed them on, and nobody ever knew. And the guys were really fired up when they saw them.

The "Mercer" stayed the same way because it was black on black, and that was fine. But the numbers had pressed-on orange numbers over them, and it was a big-time relief for me. Being in charge of a group of guys who finally got something done, we didn't want to look like a rag-tag group. We wanted them to feel good about the way they looked, and my guys were so fired up about the look and what we were wearing because they didn't know we were going to be able to make it work. I didn't tell them because I didn't know if it was going to work, so I didn't want to spoil it. That was a big moment. It was a big deal, but it doesn't seem like much. But it was a big deal to us.

The big deals were just about to get even bigger.

Tip off between Mercer and Duke. This was the first game of the day in the Friday session of the NCAA Tournament. (John Domoney)

5

A GAME TO REMEMBER

Mercer thought it could win. So did its fans. Still, it was Duke, one of the nation's basketball powers. But the Bears got the job done even against long odds on college basketball's brightest stage.

Hoffman certainly thought his team could beat Duke in the NCAA Tournament, and he let his players know that.

He didn't see it as an upset, even if most everyone else involved with college basketball saw it that way.

In their head coach's way of thinking, the Bears had been here before, and they were prepared for what they were about to face. All those wins over power conference teams and the postseason success the previous two seasons—winning the CIT and winning a first-round game in the NIT—had prepared Mercer for this moment.

On this day, the Bears went out and proved they were ready, and they proved they belonged. As Hoffman recalled,

> The attitude of our team has always been not a chip on the shoulder, but there was always a belief that we could compete if we played the way we knew how no matter what. We had been successful on the road with power conference teams, even though that wouldn't necessarily be at the level of Duke year in and year out. From that standpoint, the confidence was that we felt like we could do anything. On top of that, to throw in what Gulf Coast had done before, when we felt like we were better than them anyway and had won the regular season and lost to them in the finals, and

they go to the Sweet 16, that in itself makes you believe that your league is really good and if you play the right way, you'll have a shot. And we did.

Still, was it that big of an upset? Most of the college basketball world may have thought it was, but those affiliated with Mercer did not see it that way.

The Bears closed the game strong for the 78–71 win as their experience proved too much for the Blue Devils. Mercer started five seniors and had two more seniors who played key roles off the bench.

In fact, Mercer was the only team to start five seniors in every game that season. The only time the starting lineup changed was on Senior Day when Brown and Canevari started over Coursey and Hall.

"As far as the basketball goes, it truly was the upset of the year and got the ESPY and all the attention that came with it. I get that," Cameron said. He continued:

> But if you take the starting lineups that day and strip off "Duke" and strip off "Mercer," you've got five seniors against an inexperienced group. This team was a whole lot more experienced. They've been to the postseason three years in a row. They've knocked off Alabama. They've knocked off Tennessee, Auburn, Georgia Tech. They've won against power conference teams, so they're not scared of them. And Bob Hoffman is just a genius. If you give him time, he will find a way to beat you. Ask Ole Miss, ask these other schools. He will find a way to get to you. You felt good about that. If you compare the teams and forget it's Duke and Mercer, it's really not that big of a deal.
>
> Now, if you put the jerseys back on, yeah, there was no way we should have done it. For years, I had been thinking, "If Mercer could ever get to the NCAA Tournament and get on the selection show and get on these office brackets, there are going to be a whole lot more people who know Mercer than ever would." Did I envision it would be Duke? Did I envision it would be Friday at noon when everybody was watching? No. Did I envision beating Duke? Heck, no. But it's that double-edge of yeah, it was the upset of the year with Mercer beating Duke. But if you see where they

Mercer students made their way to Raleigh, North Carolina, for the NCAA Tournament game against Duke on several buses. (Courtesy Doug Pearson)

came from and see what they had accomplished and see everything they had been through to get there, it wasn't like that.

Duke started the game strong, which was to be expected, and had an early 9–5 lead. Coursey said it took the Bears until the first media timeout to settle into the game and get over the nerves of being in the NCAA Tournament for the first time and get over the nerves of playing Duke. Others said the Bears were ready to go from the start.
    Thomas stated,

> It doesn't take long [to get settled down]. Obviously, we were very fortunate. That was our first NCAA Tournament game. I'd be lying to say that none of us were excited or nervous because we'd been waiting for years to get to that point. It's definitely an exciting time. A huge credit goes to Coach Hoffman and all the coaching staff for preparing us and giving us a great game plan. Once you run up and down the court a couple of times, at that point it's almost second nature to execute the game plan and the calls and be in the right place on defense and do what you're supposed to do on offense.

After all, the Bears had four days to prepare for Duke and another week on top of that to get ready for the bright lights of the NCAA Tournament.

"We actually didn't feel different. We had a whole week of preparation," Hall said. "The coaches did a great job with the scouting report, and we saw them as a beatable team. We saw they had weak points, and they weren't just this unbeatable team. Everyone else thought they were, because they were Duke, but we expected to beat them and win that game. We knew it was a long shot, but we had a good game plan."

The defensive game plan focused on Parker, the Blue Devils' talented freshman. As soon as he touched the ball, the Bears double-teamed him and wanted someone else to beat them. In short, get the ball out of his hands as quickly as possible and as much as possible.

Parker finished with fourteen points but made only four of his fourteen shots from the floor, while Gollon had twenty points, including making all nine of his free throws, to lead five Bears in double figures in scoring. Coursey added seventeen points, and White had thirteen, while Hall and Nwamu each had eleven.

Duke's largest lead was seven points (in the first half), and the Blue Devils led by one, 35–34 at halftime. There were nine ties and thirteen lead changes as Mercer claimed its first NCAA Tournament win in the 108-year history of the men's basketball program.

Mercer shot 56 percent (twenty-five of forty-five) from the field and had sixteen assists compared to only eight turnovers. The Bears had a 26–10 scoring advantage in the paint and made twenty-three of twenty-eight free throws, while Duke made twelve of thirteen.

Mercer made five of thirteen attempts from behind the 3-point line, while Duke was fifteen of thirty-seven (eight of twenty-one in the first half and seven of sixteen in the second half).

"Langston was unbelievable, and Jake Gollon was special that day. Anthony White hit some big shots, all of them played well," Hoffman said. As he recalled with pride,

> Early on they hit a bunch of 3s in the first half because we had decided, and we practiced it—Darious Moten had been playing as Jabari Parker in our scout-team work. He's pretty athletic—he's not Jabari, but he has some skills. What we had decided to do, because nobody else had really tried, was that no matter where

he was on the court, when he bounced it, we were going to go trap him. Even at the top of the key, no matter where he was on the floor, we were going to go trap him and get the ball out of his hands and make somebody else make a play. So, we did that [during the game against Duke], and it gave them a bunch of open 3s, and they were hitting them. You're sitting there wondering, "Maybe we shouldn't keep doing this," but we had practiced it. We decided to stick with it in the second half, and they missed some, and we got some turnovers, and it just basically took them out of what they were doing.

It helped us with confidence and our guys thinking the plan could work. We had a bunch of game plans through the years that had worked before against different people, and the players believed in the coaching staff, and they believed in each other that they could pull it off. Part of it was the game plan, believing in the game plan, and the other part was previous experiences in those moments, even though it wasn't to that level of moment, but in those kinds of arenas, we had success in the seasons before that.

Mercer grabbed its first second-half lead on a 3-pointer by Hall with 18:23 to play, and the game went back-and-forth for the remainder of the half. But Duke gained a little bit of control with a five-point lead with about five minutes to play.

That, however, is when Mercer's experience kicked in and took over. The Bears outscored the Blue Devils 20–8 during the final 4:52 as they showed off their usual balance and team play. Coursey had two baskets and a free throw. White had a 3-pointer, a layup, and free throws. Gollon made six free throws. And Hall added a free throw. Every player, it seemed, made the right play when it was needed and came through when the team needed them to. Mercer made twelve of fourteen free throws in the final two minutes to seal the win.

The play Mercer fans will remember the most came with less than a minute left and the Bears leading 69–66. Duke pressed the inbounds play under its own basket, and Mercer took advantage as Thomas threw a long pass to White, who got behind the Duke defense. White snagged Thomas's perfect pass and raced to the basket for a layup and a five-point lead with forty-four seconds to play.

Mercer cheerleaders get their fans fired up! (Courtesy Mercer University)

With that play came a big sigh of relief throughout the Mercer contingent and even on the Mercer bench.

"When it got to the end, and they were fouling and trapping a good bit, and we had talked about it earlier in the day, 'When they deny full court, they're going to face guard, and they're not going to put a man on the ball and deny us,'" Hoffman said. He described the strategy:

> I told Bud, who took it out for us, I said, "Bud, don't be afraid to throw it deep because you won't have anybody in front of you, and if you have Anthony open, let it go." When he made that pass and Anthony caught it and laid it up, that's when I knew it was over. Until then, I had not gotten a sense.

The funny thing is, we had talked about that exact scenario, and then it played out just like we thought it would. Bud had the guts to throw the ball, and Anthony made the finish. It was the same thing we had done all year against pressure, but I made it a point to tell Bud, "They won't have a man on the ball, and if you feel it, let it go." And he did.

Thomas said he trusted in the coaches' plan and White's ability to make the play on the other end. After that, it was just about putting the ball out there for White to make the catch.

"I didn't even realize we were up three points. I thought we had a bigger lead," Thomas said with a laugh. "We ran that same play every time, and I don't know if we ever threw that pass all year. Maybe we threw it once. But I didn't see anybody deep, and I saw Anthony's eyes light up, and I felt comfortable in my passing ability to get it there."

White was confident in his ability to make the catch and the basket to go along with it. The player who had searched for a way to fit into the program as a junior college transfer made the play that helped secure the Bears' biggest win in program history.

"That's one thing that Bud and I always did, and we worked on it in practice. 'If we make eye contact, and I look at you, I'm taking off,'" White said. "It's just ironic that we only did that one time before, and that was at East Tennessee, and that's the only other time I can remember that working for us. It's funny how the most simple thing that we had worked on during practice so many times worked on the biggest stage."

In those closing moments, the Bears started to realize exactly what they were about to accomplish. And they had a few chances to take in that environment and enjoy what was going on around them.

"There was a little vindication in that," Gollon said. He continued,

The game goes so fast that you don't often have time to sit and think or to enjoy a moment when you're playing. There was an immense feeling of vindication and joy combined, if there is such a thing, in the fact that in those closing seconds we knew the game was pretty well wrapped up. One moment in particular, I remember turning around and Langston and Bud were both behind me, and I winked at Lang just kind of subtly because he knew what I was feeling.

After six years, for me anyway, this is something that needed to happen. This is something we had been working for and stressing about and killing our bodies and our personal lives and social lives to make happen. We all struggle with girlfriends, and we all struggle with friendships. We all struggle with our parents. We all struggle in class. As much as things were joyful, you had to sacrifice a lot to try to win, so to be in a scenario where you're in a game, and you breathe for a second and think, "Wow, we're doing this. There are eleven seconds on the clock, and they can't come back anymore." That is really, really special and something you'll always remember. It was an immensely freeing feeling.

Gollon's teammates felt it, as well.

"Jake was shooting free throws, and I was in the backcourt with Langston, and we started to get that feeling that we're going to beat Duke," Thomas said.

The crowd was going crazy, and there's not enough time for them to come back. Right then, me and Lang looked at each other and just embraced. After that, it's kind of a blur of just dancing and countless interviews and all that stuff. It's almost an impossible feeling to describe.

We beat Florida Gulf Coast, and you think it can't get any better than that, and then we beat Duke in the biggest tournament in college basketball. It's an indescribable feeling for sure.

Hall agreed.

"We were down, and I looked up, and we were winning by six, and I was thinking, 'How did that happen? Oh my goodness,'" Hall said with a laugh. "You could tell by looking around at everyone's faces, and everyone was thinking, 'We're really about to do this.' We just had to hold on for a few more minutes, and we did it.

"It still gives me chills watching that game and us celebrating. Every time I watch it, I get chills to this day, and it was an amazing feeling."

It was an amazing feeling that was felt all around the Mercer program and fan base. It's something to this day that Bears fans think back on and talk about as they look back on the program's best moments.

There was a huge celebration in Raleigh, for sure, and even back in Macon, there was a large watch party on campus for the fans who couldn't make the trip. As Hoffman recalled,

> After the fact, when you hear everybody tell the story of where they were when they watched the game, all over the country, all over the world, really, and then mainly the one that is fun to me is how many teachers in Macon and Warner Robins and in the area let their students stop and watch the game. They showed the game, or they listened to it or whatever. When I hear those stories, it gets you excited that there was one thing when you have a diverse city like most are in the country, but you have one thing that can get everybody excited to pull for one thing instead of pulling in different directions, that they were all cheering for us, that's exciting. I don't think anybody would have let us know where they were watching the game if we had lost . . . . I think it was more because we won and where they were when the game was going on.

Jeremy Timmerman and his wife, Jessi, are both Mercer alumni. They weren't able to make the trip to Raleigh for the game but watched from home as the minutes ticked away on the biggest win of their alma mater's history.

"When we were there, Mercer had a few big wins like at Southern Cal in 2007, but they never seemed to seal the deal when it mattered," Timmerman said. "That day, my wife and I are watching this game at our house in South Carolina, and we're going absolutely nuts in the living room, screaming and yelling. Our oldest son, Ray, was about a year-and-a-half at the time, and he didn't know what was going on, but he knew it was exciting. Kid just started yelling and hitting the couch."

Mercer fans remember that game and where they were when the victory was complete. And they certainly remember the celebration and the whirlwind that was to come.

No one can forget that.

Jake Gollon had 20 points and five rebounds against Duke. (John Domoney)

6

A MOMENT NO MERCER FAN WILL FORGET

As the final minutes ticked away, what happened on and off the court.

When it was over, Mercer celebrated, and the nation took notice. Beating Duke, a program that is widely loved and hated at the same time, certainly helped shine the spotlight on Mercer.

In the closing minutes of the Bears' thrilling win over Duke, Mercer athletics director Jim Cole said he was told to get ready for the ride.

And what a wild ride it was.

"We knew it was big because it was Duke," Cole said. "We have always heard you either love Duke, or you hate Duke. We saw that firsthand."

The Bears danced like they had never danced before. Their fans—in Raleigh and back home in Macon—celebrated like they had never celebrated before.

And the college basketball world watched it all.

After all, the win came against *Duke*. And it came in the NCAA Tournament's second round (starting in 2011, the first four play-in games were designated as the first round). On top of that, the upset occurred in the first game of the day Friday in one of the most-watched windows of the tournament each year.

It was the perfect orange and black storm, and Kevin Canevari was at the eye of the storm.

The senior guard from North Carolina broke out his version of the Nae-Nae, a popular dance and song at the time, and his teammates surrounded him. Mercer fans took it all in, all of them: the ones just a few feet away, the ones celebrating in the rest of the arena, the ones packed together for watch parties back home, and even those around the nation.

"It was definitely a spur-of-the-moment thing. When we won at Ole Miss, we had a similar dance circle, and everyone was getting in it. I got in it and just did a crazy dance," Canevari said of his Nae-Nae, which took over the sports world after his team's win. He continued,

> When we beat Gulf Coast, it was not really a dance circle, but everyone was getting rowdy. But it definitely was not on that level of what happened after the Duke game or specific to the Nae-Nae, but we just had fun dance circles. That song was just so popular at the time, and it just kind of happened.
>
> Just pure elation. It's just one of those things that you've got to realize, it's a culmination of work throughout your whole basketball career, from when you're a little kid and into rec leagues and going through middle school and high school, and you go to camps and AAU [the Amateur Athletic Union]. It's just the pinnacle, for me anyways, and just so many things are going through your head. The main thing for me was just wanting to be around my teammates. As soon as the final buzzer went off, I just sprinted out there and was hugging Darious Moten and Anthony White Jr. and just the whole team, and it was just a great moment.

In that moment, however, Canevari wasn't aware just what a national sensation he was about to become. After all, he played six minutes and didn't score during the game.

"We got in the locker room, and there is a certain time before they bring in the media," he said. He continued:

> So, I went in the bathroom, and when I came out there were like a billion cameras in my face. I was like, "I guess I played okay, but why is everyone wanting to talk to me like this?" But then they obviously started asking questions about it, and that's when I first realized it. And my phone, it was an older phone at that time, but it kept dying because all of the notifications and everything

from people calling and texting me. That's when I knew how crazy things were.

Crazy, indeed, but not really that unexpected from the players on the team. "The story is somewhat larger than the game itself," Gollon said with a laugh. As he recounted,

> Sometimes the meaning behind it can be lost, and the aftermath was awesome. That embodied our team. That's all part of the story. How many different teams on this planet, even if it's not that large of a stage, are like that when one guy starts dancing like that, and the whole team joins in? A lot of teams don't have that. There's just something about the collective spirit that it makes sense, "Oh Kevin's dancing again. Let's do it." It's not the first time we've seen him dance. It was just the best time.

Canevari said he received "calls from people I haven't talked to since I was a little kid," and that was a common theme throughout the team.

White said his phone's battery was at 98 percent when he last checked it before pregame warm-ups. It was dead after the game from all the texts and calls he received and the notifications from Twitter, Instagram, and Facebook. He wasn't able to check his phone until the team got back to the hotel. As Hall described his experience,

> My social media, my text messages, everything went crazy. I had hundreds and hundreds of texts, and I was like, "I can't respond to all this." I had about 100 missed calls, and I was thinking, "What is going on?" I thought ten or twenty people would text me, "Congratulations" or "Great job," but I literally had hundreds of texts. It was unbelievable all the support we got from Macon to people I went to elementary school with to high school to people from Atlanta. I felt like every single person I had known sent me a text or called me that day.

During the craziness that ensued and as the years have gone on, Coursey said he can't remember many specifics about the win. As he related,

53

Honestly, I can barely remember the last half of that game. For some reason, but I don't know why. I do remember some specific moments of the game but not much. I remember looking up and seeing my parents going crazy and the students going crazy and thinking, "Oh wow, we are going to win this game." And in the atmosphere of the game, I was thinking, "Okay, this might be a big deal and make ESPN and be a headline," but afterwards, when people were texting me and we were all over the highlights, I thought, "Wow, this is a huge deal."

Brown doesn't remember much about the game either but for a much different reason. He suffered a concussion during the game and wasn't able to play in the next round—an 83–63 loss to Tennessee the following Sunday.

I don't remember a ton after the game because of the concussion and because I was out of it. I understood what was going on, but the excitement for me, I had to force it a little bit because you know what's going on, but mentally you're not really yourself. That was very disheartening. You never want to have a pessimistic outlook and say, "What if?" But your mind just can't help but go there. In the back of my mind, I'm thinking, "Did I just play the last game of my college career and end it the way I wanted to?" But at the same time, I had confidence in my teammates and confidence that, "Hey, we're going to win, and I'll get past the concussion protocol, and I'll be on the slate for the next game. We'll make things happen." Unfortunately, we didn't have a great game and didn't do enough to pull it out, but the win over Duke certainly was huge for us.

The rest of the day was huge as well, as the attention remained directly on the Bears. There were the usual postgame celebrations and media responsibilities that went along with any win, but there were also national obligations and celebrations as the nation tried to figure out where and what Mercer was and how exactly it beat Duke.

That followed the Mercer team as it headed to a postgame meal after things had settled down...just a bit.

"Everybody was talking about where to go, and the guys liked Cheesecake Factory, and that's where we ate after we beat Florida Gulf Coast on the way home because it was an afternoon game, and we drove all the way home from that game," Hoffman said. He continued,

> That night after the Duke game, that's where they wanted to go, so [director of basketball operations] Jonathan Howard makes the reservations. We get all set up, and we go back and shower, and it's just amazing.
>
> The cool thing is, we get to the restaurant, and we're walking up to the restaurant, and all the sudden these girls, young girls, probably middle school or high school kids, come running forward, and I thought, "Man, what in the world?" I thought they'd be running toward Langston or Jake or the guys who played really good. And they go running right to Kevin and wanted pictures with Kevin. It had already been out everywhere him dancing, and they wanted a picture with Kevin. Right then, I knew how different and how unbelievable what had just happened [was and how] completely different than just winning a game.

There were certainly plenty of things that made that day special for the Mercer team.

Among those was the reaction by Duke head coach Mike Krzyzewski, who congratulated the Mercer coaches and players in the postgame handshake line. Then the Blue Devils legend took that a step further by going to the Bears' locker room after the game to again congratulate the team.

"They're men," Krzyzewski told the *Washington Post* that day. "They're strong, and I don't just mean physically. They have a great coach. Honestly, what they did was beautiful to see. I applaud them, and I applaud their fans for what they've done this season."

Krzyzewski wasn't the only one who applauded the Bears that day as the team became a national sensation. He may have been one of the most famous, but he definitely had plenty of company in recognizing just what Mercer accomplished that Friday afternoon.

Mercer's bench eyeing the scoreboard during the closing minutes of the game. (John Domoney)

7

A WHIRLWIND FOR THE BEARS

Mercer took the college basketball world by storm with its win over Duke, and the nation noticed. The ESPY, the trip to ESPN, and more. Coach Hoffman shares the lessons he's learned from the win over Duke, the reaction to it, and the aftermath of that crazy day.

In the midst of all the excitement, the Bears had another game to play in less than forty-eight hours, a game they ended up losing to Tennessee to end their storybook season. As Hoffman recalled,

> Going back, Lord willing I get another chance to do that, but I probably would do something different with the phones because all of ours were blowing up so much. If I could have, I probably would have done something with that because everybody wanted to talk to them. I probably should have protected them a little more, but they were good, and we had a good practice. It went good. We had people cheering us when we walked out to go practice and cheering us when we walked back, and they were cheering us to go eat and cheering us for whatever. I was going out for a walk, and they were like, "Hey! Good job!" I'm like, "I'm just going out for a walk, nothing special." But it was incredible. Those are amazing memories.

Hoffman tried to let the players enjoy the rest of the day Friday, but he and his coaching staff were already working on Tennessee, which had beaten Massachusetts in the game after Mercer's win over Duke.

Mercer, remember, had defeated Tennessee the year before in the NIT, and Hoffman thought in retrospect that this hurt his team. It also didn't help that Brown missed the game after suffering the concussion against Duke. That hurt Mercer's defense on talented Tennessee post player Jarnell Stokes, who took advantage by scoring seventeen points and grabbing eighteen rebounds. As Hoffman stated,

> Tennessee was really, really good, and they played great. We didn't have Monty, who had a concussion and couldn't play. The year before, Monty was able to play Stokes one-on-one in the post, and we didn't have to double-team him. We didn't have anybody who could play him in the post, so we were having to trap him, and they were hitting 3s better than they had hit them [during the season].
>
> I was pulling for Massachusetts when I was scouting after our game because they played right after us [and] because I knew Tennessee would be ready. Massachusetts was different because they hadn't played us and wouldn't have a feel for us, and that really makes things different.
>
> I think we should have won the game. Everybody talks about the other, and that's great, but we were good enough to win that [Tennessee] game

Hoffman says that loss, which ended his team's season with a 27–9 record, still eats at him. After all the positives of that season—he still remembers them all, for sure—that game is one he wishes he had back.

"Definitely. I'm just a crazy coach. If you don't win the last game, you're always thinking about what you could have done better," he said.

Still, there isn't much the Bears could have done better throughout that season. They shared the A-Sun regular-season title with Florida Gulf Coast and then exorcised their demons in the A-Sun Tournament against the Eagles for the conference title.

And then they beat Duke for the program's first-ever NCAA Tournament win.

All the while, the Bears put Mercer on the map as sports fans all across the nation rushed to their computers to learn as much as they could about the team and the school.

The "What is Mercer?" and "Where is Mercer?" questions that had hounded the school and program for years were all answered with that one win.

As Brown stated,

We were happy that it happened for Mercer. We found out the Mercer website crashed because so many people were looking up Mercer, and that was exciting for us. We all came to the school, and we loved the school, we loved each other, and we loved the coaches, and we value Mercer and Macon. To see all these people thinking, "What's Mercer?" to where they want to go look it up and see it's this private school and has great academics and a great law school and find out everything about us, that was great for us to know we gave back to this school that has given us so much.

The coaches and president and the university have done so much for us. We told them we wanted to be successful, and they asked what we needed, and we told them, and they came through for us. It was awesome to be able to do it for the school and not just the basketball team.

There was a big celebration for the team when it returned to Macon after the loss to Tennessee, and those warm feelings continued through the rest of the spring.

Coursey said all the students from one of his classes (he thinks it was a biology class) were at the win over Duke, and the members of the class gave him a poster board that they all signed.

"It wasn't at a big-time university where there are 60,000 students and you don't know anybody," Coursey said.

Everywhere I went, everybody knew about it, and they were going nuts about it, and it was cool. Those people got to brag about Mercer, and on a national stage, everybody knew who we were.

It picked up speed after the game, and then it picked up speed as the months went on, and it was like, "Wow, this is an enormous thing that we did." Even now, I don't know that I fully comprehend it and appreciate it.

The appreciation continued for some time. Canevari got a tour around the ESPN campus in Bristol, Connecticut, and even showed some of the sports network's anchors how to do the Nae-Nae he became famous for after the win over Duke.

"That was amazing, too. That happened so quick," he said. "Jemele Hill and Michael Smith tweeted at me, and we tweeted back at them, and then the next thing I know, I'm on their show. It was a really cool experience to just represent Mercer and be on ESPN. They showed me around the campus, and it was just an amazing experience."

The amazing experiences also included that summer's ESPY awards, with the Bears winning for "Best Upset." The players also got to hang out with some of the top athletes in the world, including NBA stars Kevin Durant and Russell Westbrook and NFL stars Richard Sherman and Von Miller.

As Gollon shared,

Any time you get the chance to be around world-class athletes or anyone at that kind of level who do anything, Hollywood has its downfalls for sure, but most people at that level who try to accomplish something like that work so hard for it, and they are so focused. When you get to be around those people and to socialize on a personal level, it's special. To be in that environment where everybody lets their guard down and to know that you're there for a reason—everyone there, there's an understanding that amid all the chaos going on outside these walls, everyone here understands with all that craziness, they're working for something meaningful, and the ones who accomplish it get to come inside those doors, there is a lot of gratification in that. Even though what we did was on a smaller scale, we got to be a part of that elite group or fraternity of people that performs like this, that takes their lives and personal goals and ambitions and makes it a No. 1 priority. Just being in an environment where you really have to dedicate yourself to earn it and it paid off in a group of people like that was pretty darn neat.

ESPN requested the use of the front page of The Telegraph *during its opening of "SportsCenter" after Mercer beat Duke. (Courtesy Daniel Shirley)*

For Thomas, a Colorado native, it was especially exciting to talk to Miller, a defensive star for the Denver Broncos, for about thirty minutes:

> The ESPYs were several months later, so it was kind of funny to have to get back in the mindset of "We beat Duke." When we beat them, we knew it was going to go down in the history books. At the time, we all told each other going in that we were going to make the most of it and go up to anybody and everybody we saw. We were right there with some of our idols for sure. You basically get treated like you're top of the world for sure.
>
> I remember checking in, and we told them we were Mercer, and the employees and the staff, they were acting like they had been waiting for us to get there and like we were one of the headline groups. You're surrounded by the best athletes in the world, but we had an easy in. When we'd introduce ourselves, we just

had to say, "We're the team that beat Duke." That was basically all it took.

Hall almost didn't make it to the event. He was taking part in the NBA's summer league with the Miami Heat and had games to play as he tried to make a name for himself and work his way onto an NBA roster.

One of his teammates, Shabazz Napier, was also nominated for an ESPY, and he got permission from the team to leave Las Vegas and head to Los Angeles for the event, and then Hall followed suit. "I didn't think it would look good if I left the team to go to the ESPYs," he said with a laugh.

> But Shabazz was on my team, and we were both invited to the ESPYs, and he talked to the assistant coach, and he said, "This is like a once-in-a-lifetime thing, so for sure go." And he told me I should go, too. So at the last minute, the day before the ESPYs, I flew to LA, and I had to go buy a suit. It was an amazing thing. To walk down the red carpet, and you see it on ESPN and see all these great athletes, it was crazy. But then to actually win the ESPY? We went to the after party, and we had the ESPY with us, and we had superstars like Von Miller asking to take pictures with us and asking to hang out with us.

That's a lot for young athletes to take in. Just a few months before, people had to ask, "What's Mercer?" or "Where's Mercer?" Now the Bears were at the middle of the sports world as they stood on stage and were honored for their win over Duke almost four months after the game took place.

"That was just one of the most fun times I've ever had," Canevari said. "We felt like a bunch of rock stars. We were just college graduates, and we were at one of the biggest events in sports. You're at all these parties and events and everything that's going on, and there are all the most famous athletes in the world, and they're all wanting to hang out with us? That's crazy."

8

THE SPECIAL SEVEN

Mercer's team was led by seven special seniors who went through so much to get to that season, coming up short a couple of times before reaching that breakthrough moment. How they led the team and how that season remains special to them to this day.

They came from all across the country, but the seven seniors from the 2013–14 season will be remembered as one history-making group.

Jake Gollon was part of the program the longest, sticking it out through six years, including two seasons battling injuries. He was tough and a heck of a do-everything player.

Langston Hall could have been an offensive star, but he instead played the role of ultimate point guard. Whatever the Bears needed on any individual night, he typically came up with.

Bud Thomas was a terrific shooter and defender, an all-around talent who played big roles on both ends of the court.

Daniel Coursey and Monty Brown controlled the middle, Coursey as the starting center, with Brown coming off the bench, and they made things difficult on opposing teams' players in the paint.

Kevin Canevari kept the team light, but he also was a tremendous competitor and made plays when called upon.

Of the seven, Anthony White had the shortest tenure, joining the program as a junior college transfer and playing only two seasons with the Bears. But he had a great impact on the team in that time and made big shot after big shot.

They were seven different players from different parts of the country: Hall and Coursey from Georgia (Atlanta and Savannah, respectively), Gollon from Wisconsin, Thomas from Colorado, Brown from Oklahoma, Canevari from North Carolina, and White from Indiana. But they came together to form one talented, cohesive and winning group. As Coach Hoffman stated,

> They put a program on the map that had been dormant for a while. Communication and technology are so different than in 1981 and 1985 [Mercer's previous NCAA Tournament teams], and when they went to the tournament, it completely changed the landscape of Mercer basketball. You don't have to tell people who Mercer basketball is or where you're at. They know. When I first got here, I had to tell people we were a Division I program, and that happened over and over again, even just speaking thirty miles from here. I had to make sure they knew we were Division I; they didn't know that. That didn't happen anymore after [the Duke win]. They knew who we were and knew what we accomplished and what it meant.
>
> They knew what level we were and who we were, and it was because of what those guys chose to believe in and because of what they chose that they wanted to accomplish and didn't let anything get in their way. They kept pushing, even when they didn't get it done the year before, and left their mark by winning the A-Sun Tournament and then what they did against Duke.

So, yes, they will go down as one unit—and not seven different parts of that unit—but they did all bring something different to the program. Hoffman broke them down, one by one:

#21
LANGSTON HALL

"He's Hall of Fame worthy, jersey retired, probably Hall of Fame in Atlantic Sun, Hall of Fame lot of stuff. He was a difference-maker in every aspect of our program. He was the right kind of guy doing the right kind of things all the time, and he impacted a culture in a way that some wouldn't even know how to start because of his upbringing

and his family and who he already was. But then just taking the things that we threw at him and taking them to another level, whether it was about communication or whether it was about execution or if it was about how we treat each other, how we go about practice. He made sure everybody was doing the right things all the time.

"I thought he was going to be special because he already knew how to do many of the things that were near and dear to my heart with communication. I thought he was under-recruited and thankfully so. He wanted to go to a strong academic institution, and he almost didn't come here because he wanted to go somewhere with football because he wanted to be somewhere that had football just for the weekends. His mom wanted him to go to an academic school, an Ivy League school, but we recruited him really hard, and our assistants did a great job to get him, staying on him, and I personally was involved a lot."

#15
ANTHONY WHITE

"Doug Esleeck recruited him, and he stayed on him. We kind of missed out on somebody, and we had been talking about him, and I had gone to see him, but he was still available in the spring, and he only had one scholarship offer. We were driving somewhere, and Doug said, 'You know Anthony's out there,' and I said, 'Let's call him,' and we did, and Anthony was a big boost for us.

"He was big, long, athletic, and could guard. He was a tremendous asset for us, even though he didn't play as much as he wanted to—nobody ever does—but he ended up being a big component for our team and our opportunity to win games. Prior to that, we had Travis Smith, and he was tremendous for us, and he was a JUCO [junior college] guy, too, but he had graduated. But Anthony fit in right away, and he had great work habits, and he worked tirelessly at his craft and did the things we wanted him to do and needed him to do."

#05
BUD THOMAS

"Bud was one of those guys who was a stat-filler. You wouldn't look at him and think right away, even though he was the two-time player of the year in Colorado, you wouldn't think he could do some of the

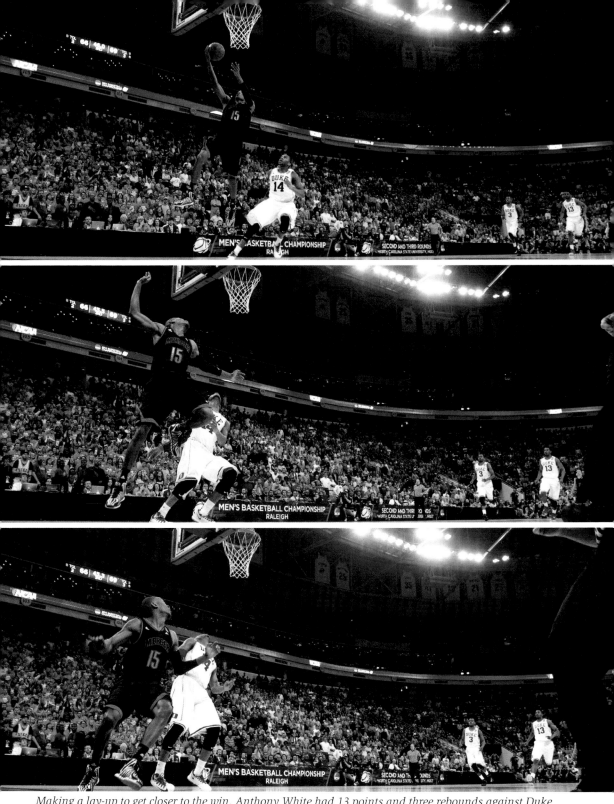

Making a lay-up to get closer to the win, Anthony White had 13 points and three rebounds against Duke. (Courtesy Mercer University)

things he could do. But his feel for the game and his understanding of running back-doors when he wasn't the quickest guy, even though he was quicker than you'd think; he had a knack for setting people up. He had a knack for scoring, a knack for rebounding. He understood the game at a high, high level, and he made us so much better when he was on the floor. He was just tremendous."

#20
JAKE GOLLON

"Six years and nine million injuries and twelve surgeries. I don't know how much it was, but it was a bunch. Everything he did that day against Duke was amazing. He had run through a tough spell that year shooting 3s, and we kept trying to get him to drive it more because he was a really good passer. Jake was the heart and soul of that team, and he had been through all six years that I had been here, so he had a different experience than the other guys and a different feel than all those guys, even the other guys who had been here four years.

"He brought forward the work ethic of James Florence and Danny Emerson and Brian Mills and those guys from the early teams; he brought all that forward, and I think that was a big deal. His maturity and how old he was and how he handled himself and how he was so well-spoken to the highest level were huge for our team."

#52
DANIEL COURSEY

"I thought I should have redshirted him; we thought about it. He had athleticism and had tools. His brother and sister had gone to Mercer, and that's why we were interested, and we knew he was a smart kid. I had seen him at our camp, and we knew he could really block shots but really couldn't do much else but hit layups every once in a while. So it was going out on a limb a little bit, but he was so big, and he had played with Langston in AAU, so we got to see them a lot together.

"I really liked him, liked his demeanor, liked his family. They were Mercer folks, so we went in on him and offered him. That was huge for us, and he really grew into a terrific player. His work ethic got better and better, as happens a lot of times with bigger guys. He grew more into his frame and his game. Right before his junior year, I told him he

Daniel Coursey had 17 points and four assists against Duke (John Domoney)

needed to change his dream because he wanted to be a doctor, which is what he's doing now. I said, 'That's fine, but if you keep working and progressing like you have, you're going to have a chance to play in the NBA. You need to dream about being in the NBA.' He said, 'Really?' And I said, 'Yes' as he was sitting right there.

"He said, 'You really think I could do that?' I said, 'You need to get after it. You've been given this gift by God and these amazing talents, and you should really push yourself.' He worked hard at it, and I think him and Monty being together really helped each other, because they were able to go at each other in drills and grow together."

#45
MONTY BROWN

"He had Harvard and other schools looking at him because he was really, really smart. We ended up recruiting him kind of sight unseen because of a recommendation of a good friend of mine who I really trusted who had coached him. When he got here, he was really skilled. He could pass. He had a really good shot. He just wasn't as athletic as Daniel, but his understanding of the game was really good. He helped us in a lot of ways. His toughness. He was farm strong, whatever you want to call it. He was just tough. If he put his mind to it, you weren't going to move him. He was just a guy, and he was going to get you.

"[Having the size of Coursey and Brown together] was huge, and in all those games we won, the Florida States, the Mississippis, Alabamas, all those different people, were because we weren't like everybody else. We were bigger. Langston was a 6-3, 6-4, at point guard, and everybody else was as big as that or bigger, so our wingspan and athleticism—we weren't the most athletic team—and our length helped us. And the smarts that they had as a team was huge. Monty could be a really,

Monty Brown scored two points in four minutes against Duke, suffering a concussion during the game. (John Domoney)

really good coach, and several of those guys could, because of their knowledge of the game. But those two [Coursey and Brown] together, pushing each other and going at it and encouraging each other, they were really good for each other. I think that came from the beginning when they were freshmen, and we wore them out doing nine million Mikan Drills a day; they got worn out. I had them every day working and trying to get better, because I knew we were going to need them and they were going to help us. And they did."

#03
KEVIN CANEVARI

"He hit some big shots and had some big moments. I knew when I saw him in high school win a state championship that his character and leadership were unbelievable. I knew if we could get him on our team—we had no scholarships available, but we were able to get that

Kevin Canevari had one assist in six minutes against Duke. (John Domoney)

done because he was a smart kid—that he was going to help our team. He impacted our team and definitely was a big component of what we were able to accomplish. If he played six minutes, he was excited about those minutes and as excited about those minutes and whatever role he could have for us."

● ● ●

Ask about the seniors, about their group, and one common word is included in the answer: chemistry. They were close as players, and they remain close to this day, getting together each summer, whether it's a cruise, a teammate's wedding or some other family event, or visiting in Savannah with the family of Jabri Bryan, who was a sophomore on the 2013–14 team but was killed during his senior season in February 2016.

"The chemistry among those guys was unbelievable. Just from a personal experience, they took care of me," Rick Cameron said with a big smile on his face. He continued,

> If we were on the road, they made sure, "Does Rick have this? Does Rick have that?" Jake always cut me a part of the nets whenever they won something and cut one down. They treated me like they were our sons. The way they meshed together, they were a unit of destiny. You could see it. They knew their role. Any successful basketball team has to have a great point guard, and Langston was the ultimate point guard. He could sense on any given night what was working and what he needed to do for us to win, and he did that. It might be him scoring. It might be, "My shot's not here tonight, and I need to dish and get eight or nine assists." It might be, "I need to play better defense against their point guard tonight."
>
> The heartbeat of that team was Jake Gollon. Jake, what he could do was just priceless. What he could do for that team on the bus, in the locker room to set the tone for that team; it's unbelievable the character that young man has.

That togetherness also reached into the Hoffman family, and not just Bob Hoffman.

"They were terrific and definitely special, and not only what they did on the court and playing games," Kelli Hoffman said. Further,

> Most of them were here all four years, with the exception of Anthony White, and he just fit right in with the rest of them. When you have a group that is here that long and you get them as freshmen, they just come in as boys, and they grow up to men the four years that they're here. Just to watch that happen in their lives is special, and they were just so close; they were like brothers. And they really treated me like a mom. I got to be close to their parents and their families.

Each of the seven has his own thoughts on the group and what made it so special and close. And a lot of that focuses on the common theme for this group: chemistry.

Langston Hall: *"We went through so much together, on and off the court. It's like a family but maybe even closer than that. Those guys knew what you went through, and you knew what they went through, and we all appreciated each other for that."*

Jake Gollon: *"The comedy, whether it be in team meetings or in restaurants or on the bus, any time our team was together, you were hard-pressed to not be laughing. I was not funny at all. I was the one laughing or getting laughed at, but I have no shame in saying that I can't tell a joke to save my life. I'm too serious all the time. But when you've got guys like Kevin Canevari, and he's just got this innate ability to put smiles on other peoples' faces, and you've got other people who love each other and understand what family is like, every scenario outside the court was equally as fun. It felt like we were always a team. We were always interacting with the team bloodlines flowing through our veins everywhere we went.*

"We have a big echo thing. One of our rules on the court was when a player called a play or the defense called a play, we all had to echo it. The gym could get loud, and if we couldn't all hear it, it would be tough. Coach Hoffman's rule is you echo it, so we're on the court and someone calls a play, 'Fist three. Fist three,' and everyone has to respond, 'Fist three. Fist three.' Well, we were at a restaurant, and the

waiter walks out with the first meal that was ready and says, 'Pork chop with mashed potatoes,' and the whole table in the middle of the restaurant as grown men, yells out, 'Pork chops with mashed potatoes.' It was so obnoxious, but it comes from such a place of joy that we just had such a phenomenal experience everywhere we went and put smiles on peoples' faces. It was a unique group."

Monty Brown: *"You have guys coming from all over the country. Bud's from Colorado. Anthony's from Indianapolis. Kevin's from North Carolina. Jake's from Wisconsin. I'm from Oklahoma. Langston and Daniel are from Georgia. You have a melting pot from guys being from all over the country, different styles of basketball and different kinds of leagues. But when you come in and you buy in, and when I say, 'Buy in,' you buy into each other, you buy into this belief that this every-day grind of struggling through workouts and almost passing out during conditioning and these thoughts of 'What did I get myself into?' and believing this is all for a bigger purpose. Coach Hoffman was our leader; he was someone we could trust and believe in, and whatever he said to us, we were going to believe that it will come true.*

"Langston's ability to be a floor general and to keep the group together in times when we weren't doing so hot and missing some shots and the other team is going on a run, his leadership was unbelievable. Jake had the ability to go to the coaches, and Langston did, too, or if the coaches called something, those guys could go back to the coaches and say, 'Hey, I was watching film, and I saw that these guys are going to do this. Why don't we do this?' And the coaches were very open to that. Maybe they wouldn't agree all the time, but they were open to listening and using things in practice and trying to figure things out. It wasn't just the coaches telling us what to do and us following. The coaches took our feedback, and that built chemistry. It's not just the players having chemistry; it's the players and the coaches working together and every single person on that team was on the same page."

Daniel Coursey: *"We were all super close. I've talked to a lot of other college basketball players who were part of a senior group, and one of them was off doing something, and another one was off doing something else with other people. It wasn't like that with us. On and off the court, we were hanging out together. On the court was like a* *minor part of it. I don't even see them as basketball players. They're just friends who I lived with and hung out with, but yeah, we played basketball together. If we need something from one of them or one of them needs something from us, it gets done."*

Bud Thomas: *"We're all very blessed to have clicked like that. Just because you're teammates and spend every day together, it doesn't mean you're all going to get along, but the fact that we did and we never got sick of each other, and if we did, we'd have a little scuffle, and then ten minutes later we're fine, it's a pretty special relationship that all of us have together. We're all very grateful for deciding to go to Mercer and how it worked out."*

Kevin Canevari: *"The character of everybody as a whole, and that stems from Coach Hoffman developing the program as a whole for the right reason. We had guys who bought into that, on and off the floor, and we had been through so much, good and bad, and been there since our freshman year. The character and care that we had for one another. Not all of us were the same personality-wise, but we jelled as a whole because we were all together for the right reasons.*

"We always have a group text that goes around daily. We still make fun of Daniel Coursey every day. We still pick fun at each other. Once a year, we all get together and try to see each other face-to-face once a year. Luckily, in today's age, it's easier to stay in touch with each other. It's not always in person, but we can stay in touch with each other, and it's a bond that will never be broken."

Anthony White: *"We're brothers in every sense of the word except we don't have the same parents. We've all argued before. We all have had our down times and our good times. We've all had tough moments. But at the end of the day, we're all there for each other, which is what makes us really cool as a group."*

SENIOR SEASON PRODUCTION

Monty Brown
Averaged 4.5 points
Season high of 16 against Oklahoma
Averaged 2.3 rebounds

Kevin Canevari
Averaged 1.5 points

Daniel Coursey
Averaged 10.1 points
Season high of 20 against Brown
Averaged 6.4 rebounds
Averaged 2.1 blocks (led conference)

Jake Gollon
Averaged 8.1 points
Season high of 37 against Valparaiso

Langston Hall
Averaged 14.6 points
Season high of 25 against Northern Kentucky
Made eight 3-pointers against Northern Kentucky
Averaged 5.6 assists (led conference)

Bud Thomas
Averaged 8.9 points
Season high of 31 against Lipscomb
Made nine 3-pointers against Lipscomb

Anthony White
Averaged 8.5 points
Season high of 29 against Jacksonville
Shot 43.1 percent from 3 (led conference)

Langston Hall and head coach Bob Hoffman review strategy during Mercer's win over Duke. (John Domoney)

9

COACH HOFF

Bob Hoffman and the win: what it meant to him then,
what it means to him now, and his thoughts on the team.

The cohesiveness of the Mercer program started at the top with its head coach. Hoffman took over the Bears' program before the 2008–09 season and faced a difficult rebuilding job.

The Bears were coming off three straight losing seasons, but in Hoffman's first season, they finished with a winning record overall and in the conference (17–15 overall and 11–9 in the A-Sun).

After a couple of losing seasons (16–17 in 2009–10 and 15–18 in 2010–11), the Bears took off with seasons of twenty-seven wins in 2011–12, twenty-four wins in 2012–13, and twenty-seven wins in 2013–14.

The 2013 and 2014 A-Sun Coach of the Year, Hoffman became the first coach in NCAA history to record a win in all four postseason tournaments (NCAA, NIT, CBI, and CIT) in a four-year span following a 72–70 win over Stony Brook in the 2015 CBI opening round.

"It's unbelievable how rock solid he is," Cameron said. He continued,

> People who know him know what a strong man of faith he is. Seriously, I know this is an old cliché that a coach changes lives and coaches people and not just players and wins and losses, but that's truly Bob Hoffman.

There are two things: how complicated his scheme is and how hard it is to pick up on it. He doesn't necessarily need a guy who is averaging forty points per game to come in; he's not going to build a system around that guy. The guys are going to have to fit into his system. Bob is so strong, and when these guys leave the program, whether they win a championship or not, they're better people. They are prepared to take on the world. They succeed in life, and that's Bob Hoffman.

The passion Hoffman coaches with on the sideline and how much he cares for his players are obvious to anyone who has been around him. He once joked that he has worn the same shoes on the sidelines for years but that he has to get new soles put on them because of his famous foot-stomp to get his players' attention—or that of the referees.

Kelli Hoffman is his wife of nearly forty years, and they have one son, Grant. Kelli knows what the game and his players mean to him, and she has seen him grow from his early days as a young coach.

"All losses are tough. He goes into every game thinking we're going to win it, regardless of who we're playing," she said. She continued,

> He's really good about balancing the emotions of being a very emotional Bob Hoffman on the sidelines. He's passionate about everything he does, whether that's coaching his guys, whether that's loving on his family, whether that's being a dad, whether that's worshiping the Lord; whatever it is, he's very passionate about what he does. When you have that kind of personality, you have to learn to really balance those kinds of emotions.
>
> If you don't, you don't make it. He learned to do that. He went from being a coach in his very early days who got up and threw up every morning of a game, every single morning. I finally said, "You have to get control of this, or you're going to have to find another profession, or this will kill you. We can't live life like this." And he did, he learned over time how to balance those feelings and emotions.
>
> He doesn't bring things home. If there are ever problems with players or coaches, I don't ever know about them, and I so appreciate that because he's just good about keeping work at work. When he comes home, he's dad, and he's "Honey," I guess you would say. He learned to balance basketball and family. It's not

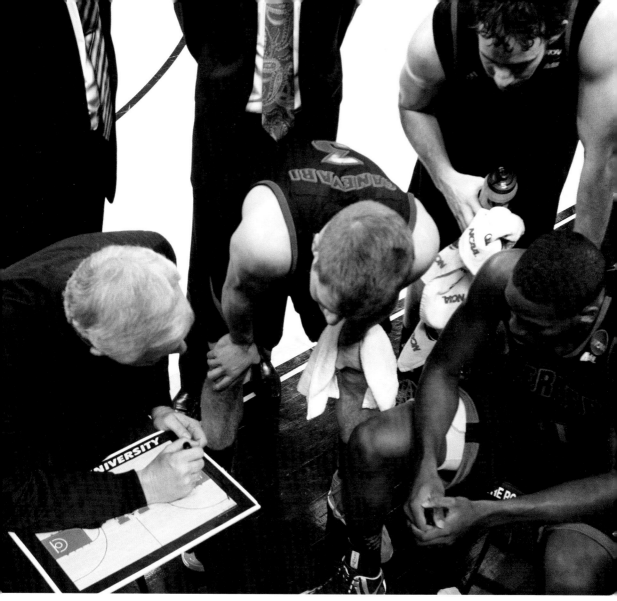

Head coach Bob Hoffman goes over strategy with his players during a timeout. (John Domoney)

that he's not disappointed after a loss, and after those losses, I just have something for him to eat and give him some space to debrief. We don't talk about it, partially because I really don't understand, but secondly I think he just needs to think through things without my input, and then he's fine with it.

Mercer baseball head coach Craig Gibson has grown close to Hoffman through the years, and Gibson also knows what it takes to build a winning program from almost nothing. He has done so with the Bears' baseball program, taking the team to the NCAA Tournament several times after taking over a struggling program.

He marvels at what Hoffman has accomplished.

"Bob's a great guy. First and foremost, he's a great person," Gibson said. Further,

> He's a guy that anyone would be satisfied to let their children play for him, and that's the highest compliment I can give Bob. I think he's a great leader on campus. He's a great leader of young people. He's a great mentor. He's a great face of our department and our university. I don't think we could have a better person as a face of our institution, and on top of that, he's an unbelievable basketball coach. For us to have Bob Hoffman here is huge. He could coach on any level. I think he could coach in any league and be successful. His basketball IQ is just phenomenal. He's a special guy. We're fortunate to have him.

Hoffman got win number 200 at Mercer on November 16, 2018, with a 77–60 decision over Tennessee-Martin. He got win number 600 of his career overall a few nights later when his team beat Maryland-Eastern Shore 80–42.

"These things are very team-oriented. I have had great players and great assistants since I have been here," he said on the athletic department's website.

> I have been blessed tremendously with an administration that wants us to be successful and gives us opportunities to be successful. Our home crowd, no matter what night it is, always brings it. So many people go into it. Our success is everybody's success. I am just grateful that Mercer gave me an opportunity several years ago. I think we still have some serious business to take care of this season, but I am very fortunate to be able to do what I love to do.

The players know just how fortunate they are to have played for him and what Hoffman means to them and their growth as players and men.

Monty Brown: *"He'll always be like a father figure to me personally, and I think the same could be said by many of the team members. The thing that sticks out for me in Coach Hoffman is his faith in Christ. I share that same faith. He showed his Christian aura through his actions, through his words, through how much he cares. He had so much going on; he's the coach, yes, but he's a father and a husband and had a family to worry about. But even with all that, if you needed something, he would say, 'If you need something, call me. My door's always open. I'm not just your coach. I'm your friend, and I'm here for you.' He's the coach, and he's the authority, and we respected that, but after practice, you could walk up to him and get a big hug and ask how each other's doing. He was close with all our families. Just a genuine spirit."*

Kevin Canevari: *"He's meant a lot because through those ages of eighteen to twenty-two, people are still becoming men and learning what life is all about, he does a great job of developing people and teaching life lessons. We had character meetings every Sunday and things like that; he had us at his house to eat dinner. If you're around him enough, you kind of start to understand where he's coming from. Having someone like that is something we're forever grateful for."*

Daniel Coursey: *"He bred that atmosphere of taking care of each other and being part of the group, and that's big in helping a team grow. I've played for coaches who have separated guys or are like, 'He's the guy we have to go to' or 'These are the guys who are scorers and everybody is a role player.' Hoffman was literally the opposite of that. He was like, 'Everybody is part of the team. We're all going to get along, and we're all going to hang out with each other. And we're all going to be close, and that's the way it's going to be.' And it just worked out well for us."*

81

Jake Gollon: *"I was a captain with Lang, and I was there for two years before he got there. Six of the other seven never saw the first two years. I have a special bond with Coach Hoffman. He gave me a long leash because I think he understood my dedication and my commitment, and then it was up to me to realize where I or the team needed improvement rather than to hold firm to a thought or to an idea. I probably argued more than I should have, and it came back to bite me. I coached for three years, and I thought daily, 'I would have hated to coach myself.' Coach Hoffman gave me a really great opportunity because I signed to play for Coach Slonaker, so technically I was there even before Coach Hoffman got there.*

"Another player in Wisconsin had also signed with Mercer, and Coach Hoffman saw him and said he would honor his scholarship but didn't think he fit the system. So the kid called me and said he wasn't going anymore, and Coach Hoffman was coming to see me. For a couple of hours, my whole world was turned upside down, and I didn't know what was going to happen. And I had already been dealing with injuries.

"I was in a really bad place mentally, not really knowing where I was headed or what I was doing. Coach Hoffman came up, and after meeting me and some of the people who were important to my life, some of the coaches in Stevens Point, he understood more about me and what was important to me. It's not always that blatant because I'm pretty introverted in a lot of ways. I can be very vocal, for sure, but I don't necessarily make things public, and I think he could feel that. From the day I stepped onto that campus, there was a lot of love that I could feel from Coach Hoffman, like a father figure, like a family member, maybe an uncle or something like that. He made a commitment and promised he would take care of me, and he did. I promised him I would give him my absolute best, and I did. Even after that, when he decided to keep me on the team, I spent two years being injured and hurt on a full scholarship. That's not good. If you're a coach, every scholarship is important, and if you don't contribute, you're on the chopping block, and I knew that. So I had to show up every day and pour my heart and soul into the rest of the team because Coach Hoffman did a good job of coaching me and telling me what I needed to do to contribute and also because I wanted to keep my scholarship. He held true to his word."

Langston Hall: *"He just knew how to get the best of everybody. He knew at times how he could coach different people. Some people you have to yell at them and go crazy. Some people you have to just talk to them. I think that helped us. Everybody just trusted him, and we all listened to him. If he said, 'Do this,' even if we might not think it was right, we did it. Every now and then, Jake might have some different ideas or a few words, but at the end of the day, he would do it. One-hundred percent Jake was the one who could express what we were thinking as players. He wouldn't talk back or anything, but if Coach said, 'Run 2, this play,' Jake might say, 'Why don't we run 1?' He wouldn't be in Coach's face or anything, but he might see it from a different perspective and inject his ideas and his way of thinking. And Coach Hoffman was okay with that because he knew how much Jake cared and how much we all cared."*

Bud Thomas: *"Not in a negative way, but he basically runs your life for four years. We were all very fortunate to have a guy like that in control of our lives for those four years. He's huge into growing you and molding you, and we experienced all sorts of stuff. I'm extremely grateful for everything he's done for me and everything he's taught me. When you see him and you're back on campus, it's like you never left. He gives you a big bear hug, and his face lights up. And even Mrs. Hoffman, we're basically like their kids for four years; you go over for Thanksgiving dinner and all sorts of stuff. We're all very lucky, and it's not a coincidence with all that we accomplished."*

Anthony White: *"His enthusiasm, to be honest. He would be too enthusiastic sometimes, and we'd just laugh. But he always kept us engaged. One thing he always preached to us was being talkative and communicating with each other, and that is probably the biggest thing that made us what we were. I'm not going to limit it to Coach Hoffman. Those assistant coaches, they always balanced it out. If Hoffman was focusing on the ref, those guys were always stepping in and letting us know what was about to happen and what we needed to do. If he was on us, and we were really frustrated, those guys would calm us down. It was a perfect mix and a perfect fit for us as players."*

HOFFMAN THROUGH THE YEARS

Southern Nazarene
(Women, Three Seasons)

Year	W–L
1987–88	21–11
1988–89	36–02
1989–90	31–03
	88–16

Texas Pan-Am *(Five Seasons)*

Year	W–L
1999–00	12–16
2000–01	12–17
2001–02	20–10
2002–03	10–20
2003–04	14–14
	68–77

84

Oklahoma Baptist
(Nine Seasons)

Year	W–L
1990–91	15–17
1991–92	16–17
1992–93	34–04
1993–94	30–07
1994–95	28–06
1995–96	29–07
1996–97	36–04
1997–98	24–09
1998–99	31–07
	243–78

Mercer
(Ten Seasons) *

Year	W–L
2008–09	17–15
2009–10	16–17
2010–11	15–18
2011–12	27–11
2012–13	24–12
2013–14	27–09
2014–15	19–16
2015–16	19–15
2016–17	15–17
2017–18	19–15
	198–145

Before 2018-19 season

Coach Hoff

10

THE MANIACS

The support Mercer's student body showed in the big win over Duke was outstanding. What did those "Mercer Maniacs" take from that experience and what do they think about it as they look back on it?

Jim Cole expected the Mercer basketball team—and its fans—to be walking into a hostile environment for the game against Duke.

After all, Raleigh is just about twenty-five minutes from Durham, and it is more than 400 miles from Macon to Raleigh. Plus, it's *Duke*. There would have to be tons of Blue Devils fans at the game, right? Duke is the powerhouse everyone wants to see, and the Blue Devils' fans would be there to support their team in full force, right?

Well, it turns out the atmosphere was more hostile for the Blue Devils than the Bears. Sure, a lot of folks dislike Duke, so the other teams' fans would lean toward Mercer—and that lean became stronger the more it looked like Mercer could win—but plenty of credit has to be given to the Mercer administration for getting the Mercer students, band, cheerleaders, dance team, and yes, Toby the mascot, to the game to cheer on the Bears.

And Hoffman's team noticed from the time the players ran on the court for the pregame warm-ups. As he remembered,

> The crowd was actually more our crowd than Duke, which was amazing, and we were appreciative that the president and our administration and leadership pulled that off. There was no way not to know. I think on TV and everywhere else, they commented

on it several times. It was almost embarrassing. If we were playing twenty minutes from here or thirty minutes from here, you would hope we would have a good crowd. I think the deal was it was midafternoon, and they had won so much and done so much and Coach K was amazing, which he is still unbelievable, that they figured they were going to get through that round and spend their money on the next game or the Final Four.

There were other teams' fans in the building, as normally happens in those settings, and all the other fans, they were cheering for us. That added to the feel that it was all Mercer when it was other teams' fans getting involved, but it was certainly special to see all those Mercer fans there, and what our folks were able to do to get them there was amazing.

What it took to get them there adds to the story.

Carrie Ingoldsby, working with the Campus Life group, said the school lined up seven buses to take the students to the game against Duke (that number climbed to ten for the game against Tennessee), and she sat in the front of a bus for both rides.

"The energy coming off the bus was really fun, the march to the arena and getting in there was really exciting and being a part of that is something we'll never forget," she said. "Of course, I'm in the background trying to make sure everything is running the right way. 'Did everyone get their tickets? Are we parked in the right place? Did everyone get a shirt?' There were a lot of details going on that we were trying to make sure were checked off. Once we got them there and got them in, it was just like, 'We did it,' and it was a huge sigh of relief."

Cindy Strowbridge was the assistant director of Campus Life at the time, and she said there were 360 students on the buses for the Duke game (and close to 600 for the Tennessee game).

The buses went up Thursday for the game against Duke and made the return trip to Macon after the game. As soon as the Duke game was over, Ingoldsby, Strowbridge, and others went right to work on getting buses set up for the return trip to Raleigh for the game against Tennessee.

"We walk in, and I think it was overwhelming to the other fans who were in there. We came in there in full force, and we just overwhelmed the security force a little bit," Strowbridge, a Mercer gradu-

Fans watching at Mercer Village react during the final seconds of the Duke game. (Courtesy Mercer University)

ate, said of the Duke game. "We had all rode the buses over there together, and we all came in and were getting seated. There were Duke fans milling around, and I don't think they knew what to expect when they saw this flood of orange coming in. That's something they will remember for years, I'm sure."

President Bill Underwood wanted the Mercer students close to the floor (and not to be relegated to the nosebleed seats) to give the team an extra boost, and many of the program's boosters gave up their seats close to the floor so that could happen.

Some of the students even snuck down closer from their seats and squeezed in to be closer to the action.

"The Big Ten office called us because they saw what the scene was on TV," Underwood said.

> The usual thing is to put the students in the cheap seats where Duke had their students sitting, and you couldn't even see them sitting up there. Our decision to put the students in the best seats on the floor was part tactical and part philosophical. One, it was a great opportunity to say in a very visible way what our institu-

tion is about: the students come first. Secondly, the students were going to be a lot louder than the rest of us, and they might actually give our team a boost. I think they actually did.

It certainly paid off for the Bears.

"We were in Raleigh playing Duke, but it felt like we were the home team," Thomas said. "I'm sure we had our fair share of Duke haters helping us, but those students were awesome, and having that support and seeing all those folks and the sea of orange was special."

The players heard the "Mercer" and "Bear" chant going through the crowd and noticed when the students began their "I believe that we will win!" cheer right before tipoff. That cheer had become a home game tradition with the Mercer Maniacs student group, along with throwing streamers in the air during the cheer.

Even the streamers snuck their way into the arena, although that's not permitted at NCAA Tournament games. Security was ready for that for the game against Tennessee.

Canevari remembers the Mercer lacrosse team, which had a game in the area, being in the stands.

"They didn't even have good seats. They were in the nosebleeds, and you could tell they were going crazy up there," Canevari said of the lacrosse players. "A lot of those guys were my friends, and it was cool to see that kind of commitment. Even Coach Hoffman said something about that."

Jeremy Timmerman graduated in 2008, with Hoffman arriving in his final weeks as the editor of *The Cluster*, the campus newspaper. In the years Timmerman was at Mercer, there were very few in attendance at most home games other than a few rows of students and a sparse crowd elsewhere in the arena.

"You could get there twenty minutes before the game or something like that and get the 'first fan in the game' bonus," he said. "But that meant a free pizza and sitting in a pair of recliners at the other end of the arena, and there was nobody down there. So, you'd just take the pizza."

Canevari also remembers the change in the student support for the program during his time with the Bears. Mercer basketball was not a hot ticket in Hoffman's early years. That changed with the team's success and the arrival of the A-Sun Tournament in Macon.

"Freshman year to senior year was a full 180," Canevari said. "Our freshman year, Hawkins Arena would not be very packed. By the time we graduated, we had a lot of sellout games, and the games were just different. That's a testament to Coach Hoffman and our program and what we were able to accomplish and the students appreciating that and wanting to be a part of it."

The students certainly wanted to be part of something special, and Hoffman and the Bears were building something special.

Justin Baxley was a freshman during the 2013–14 season, and his grandfather had been diagnosed with cancer earlier in 2013. Baxley was looking for something to take his mind off the seriousness of life and found it with that team.

"Sports can help you get through a lot in life. At the time, I was going through a lot, and I kind of latched onto the team," said Baxley, who said the first game he attended was against Seton Hall in November.

> I had really given up watching sports, and I just said at the time that sports wasn't for me. I no longer wanted to think about sports because that was my connection to [his grandfather], and you realize he's going to be taken away from you, and I pretty much stopped watching sports altogether.
>
> My friends dragged me to the Seton Hall game that year with Mercer, and for the first time in months, I was able to get what was going on in my life off my mind. From that moment, I was like, "I have to go to every game now," and I went to every home game. This is my time away from everything that was going wrong. That team gave me an escape from everything for forty or fifty minutes when they were playing.

That connection between the students and players continued through the Raleigh trip.

"That entire week leading up to that game Friday, I was nauseous. I couldn't concentrate. I couldn't focus," said Jane Heeter, who was a junior that season. She continued,

> We went up Thursday and came back Friday night. I remember we were on a charter bus, and they had TVs on there, and I couldn't even watch what was on. I was such a mess the entire time because

Mercer students made their voices heard during the Bears' upset over Duke. (John Domoney)

I was excited and nervous and scared because I thought we actually had a chance to win, which made it worse. If we had been a sixteen seed and playing a team we knew we were going to lose to, it would have been easier. But in my mind, I was thinking, "We can win this game. We can actually win."

Once we got there to the arena, we could see the arena, and we could see this sea of orange coming from us getting off the buses with the students, the faculty, and staff. We took a picture all together outside the arena, and we were all screaming and yelling. It became real then and completely terrifying.

Thomas Norton, a sophomore that season, had been a Duke fan in middle school and high school, but those allegiances changed when he became a Mercer student. And there were plenty of good vibes about the Bears' chances around the campus leading up to the game.

"The week leading up to the game, the whole week before the game, usually when you get this kind of matchup, it's like, 'Hey, we made the tournament; that's what matters,'" he said. "But just the atmosphere around campus was, 'Hey, we're going to win. Yes, it's Duke, but we can win this game.' Everyone was really positive and optimistic for the game." He continued,

> On the bus ride up there, everyone was really excited and doing chants. When we got there, the realization that this was coming together felt surreal. It was just this sea of orange. I was one of the first ones off the bus, and when you looked, there was just this line of orange marching toward the front of the arena. I don't think anyone expected that kind of presence from a small school like Mercer. I knew we had great fans, and I knew we had a lot of people on the buses, but when you see it all in person and see all those people there together, it's overwhelming, honestly. It's something you love to see, that kind of support for the team.

Justin Furness, a freshman that season, found his way to the front row amid that sea of orange.

"I just remember being ready, ready to get into the stadium and watch the game and see how it would play out," he said. "Everybody was asking us, 'Who are you? Who's the orange team? Are you guys Chattanooga?' 'No, we're not Chattanooga.' We kind of took the city by storm, and everyone knew who we were after that."

They certainly did, and sports fans from all around the country were trying to reach anyone and everyone affiliated with Mercer during the game, especially in the closing minutes when it looked like the Bears would win.

"During the game, my Twitter was blowing up because for years, I had been live tweeting Mercer basketball games, and I had become friends with BYU fans from when we played out there in the NIT and other teams, too," Heeter said. "A lot of people who had no connection to Mercer knew me and were tweeting me, and I'm just like, 'I can't respond right now, my God.'"

Dean of Students Doug Pearson was on one of the buses for the trip to Raleigh. He had a quick speech for the students on his bus as it pulled out of the parking lot at Mercer.

"I said, 'You guys behave, and I'm in charge of this bus, blah, blah, blah,'" he said with a laugh. "Then I said, 'I'm picking the first movie on the way up,' and I said, 'We're watching *Hoosiers*.' That was what we had to watch, right?"

Yep, the small school taking out the big powerhouse program. It was a perfect selection, and after the Bears pulled off their version of *Hoosiers*, the reaction was one of elation from the Mercer students and fans and surprise from the other teams' fans.

"Everyone was just hugging everybody, and you didn't even know who they were. It was just like you won the lottery, and it was such euphoria, and it was just so wild," Pearson said.

> We were leaving the arena after the game, and people were coming up to us asking, "Where is Mercer University?" "What is Mercer?" That's what you want. That's an admissions person's dream, and it was just incredible. Everybody just felt like something special had just happened, and you knew it. People all over the country were calling me and leaving me messages on the phone. "Are you there? What's going on? You're blowing up my bracket!"
>
> We got back early morning, and it was so quiet on the bus because everyone was asleep and burned out. I grabbed the mic again, and I told them, "All right, come on, let's go," and they were all getting moving. I told them, "I've been to two national championship games and have been doing this a long time, but what you just experienced was the best moment ever." I said, "Keep your tickets because people are going to claim they were there, and you were."

Baxley was happy he was there, and he enjoyed the interactions with the other fans before and after the game.

"These two guys walk up, and I had no idea who they were. They tell me they needed a reason to root for Mercer. They're North Carolina fans, and one of them, his words to me were, 'Tell me why Mercer is going to win,'" he said.

So I went on this long rant about how Bud Thomas can hit twenty-five 3s in a row in shoot-around and never miss, about Jake having this illustrious career, Langston is an all-around great point guard, he plays the game the right way. We have some big-time defenders in Coursey and Monty off the bench giving us size. So I went on this long thing, and that came after thinking the whole ride up there that we have no chance to beat Duke, that it's not even possible. I really went on this trip because Coach K is a legend, and I wanted to see an NCAA Tournament game in person. Even in my bracket, I picked Duke to win and had them going to the Final Four, I think.

So I start rattling off all this stuff to these random guys, and I started to think, "Wait a minute, maybe we *can* win."

After the win, the fun with the other fans continued for Baxley and the other Mercer students.

"After the game, I had people walking up to me trying to give me $40 and $50 to buy the shirt off my back. They would do anything to get Mercer stuff," he said. "These were North Carolina fans, and they wanted to buy a towel, anything they could get; they would buy it because we beat Duke. We had people walking up and thanking us for beating Duke and knocking them out of the tournament.

"One guy walked up and said, 'I'll give you $50 for that shirt.'

"I said, 'You mean the one I'm wearing?'

"He said, 'Yep, I just want Mercer stuff.'"

Rick Cameron, from his spot on press row, certainly had a good look at the Mercer contingent before, during, and after the game.

When the game was over, and we concluded the postgame, and the game after ours was warming up, somehow we had ended up on the upper concourse, and it was forty-five minutes or an hour after the game, however long it had been, so it's time to go load the bus. To get on the bus, we had to come back down to the floor on the far side, walk on the floor, and then go out the other side, and as we do that, our students are still hanging around in the arena, and they start chanting because the players were back in the arena. And the other fans, anybody not Duke, picked up on it and started cheering for our guys, too. Everybody was coming to their feet, and our guys were coming down, and we almost had a parade going down through the arena, and they got a standing ovation from everyone there.

That was a long time coming for the university, and Cameron enjoyed every minute of it.

"I never had seen the Mercer students in unison, join in, and enjoy something like that of, 'Hey, we're a legitimate Division I deal,'" he said. "The pride that they had, and everyone had their 'Mercer Way' shirts on to show their pride. It was a new day for the Mercer students of, 'Hey, we can go across the ticker on the bottom of the screen just like the big boys and be a national, credible institution, and we're not just little ole Mercer any more.'"

11

MAKING THE MOST OF THE MOMENT

What did the win over Duke mean for the Mercer program and the university as a whole? How have the basketball program, the athletics department, and the university grown from that moment and used it to market the university?

There is a clear line in the sand for Mercer as a university before March 21, 2014, and after March 21, 2014.

Sure, it was "just sports" or "just a game," but that day certainly helped change Mercer. It changed the athletics department, for sure, and it made a difference in the university as a whole.

And that was a big part of Bill Underwood's plan when he took over as the school's president.

"The old saying is that sports is the front porch to the university," he said. "That game illustrates that. That game did more for our profile than anything else we could have done. That showed what the power of sports is, in terms of bringing people together, thousands of people out here sitting and watching the game on the big screen on our campus, thousands of people in North Carolina for the moment. Sports just build communities in a way that nothing else can."

That was easy to see around the Mercer campus after that win. Something changed. Something was different.

There was a different energy around the campus, and it can still be felt to this day.

Bob Hoffman, left, Jake Gollon, Langston Hall, Bud Thomas and Anthony White meet with the press after the win over Duke. (John Domoney)

"It was a very proud moment, kind of an indescribable feeling and something that I don't think a lot of us will experience again, that type of elation or just pure joy and seeing our student-athletes working so hard and our students cheering for and supporting a school that we all love," Strowbridge said. "It is a memory that I will never forget, the students who were there will never forget, the alumni will never forget. The last part of the semester that year was just a sense of we are Mercer—and that was our chant 'We are Mercer'—and it was just a feeling that we were together, and that's wonderful to be part of."

Yes, sports can be that powerful, and the numbers back it up.

University spokesman Larry Brumley described what the leaders of the university call the "Duke Effect."

He said the overall university enrollment in the fall of 2013—pre-Duke—was 8,316. The figure in the fall of 2017 was 8,667, an increase of 351 students, or 4.2 percent. He also pointed to the university's Macon undergraduate enrollment as an even bigger indicator of the effect the Duke win had on the university.

In the fall of 2013, that number was 2,554, but by the fall of 2017, it had grown to 3,253, which is an increase of 699 students, or 27 percent.

Again, it was part of the plan and vision Underwood had for the athletics department and the university as a whole. During that same period, Mercer was adding a football program, originally a non-scholarship program that later added scholarships.

That new football program helped pave the way for Mercer's athletics teams to move from the A-Sun to the Southern Conference, officially joining the conference on July 1, 2014. But the ascension of Hoffman's program played a big role in that also.

"When the Southern Conference was looking to add someone, what they saw in Mercer was a good academic institution with an upwardly mobile basketball program that was willing to play scholarship football. And we had the geography, too," Underwood said. "They wanted a presence in Georgia, and we had all those things. We were admitted into the league before the Duke win, but I think they could see the trajectory we were on. In fact, they told me they could."

After the win over Duke, the folks around the Mercer program and the school in general saw a different focus and attitude about their university. People now knew Mercer, knew where it was, knew what it was, and knew what it could accomplish.

Craig Gibson sees it. Yes, he has a successful baseball program in its own right, but he knows the basketball team's win over Duke was a moment of change for the university.

97

> Wow, I think it's hard to sort of quantify what that team meant to all of us. That team, just in the department, helped set the bar high for the rest of the teams. Just certainly a tangible goal to get on the national stage, that meant a lot. From the university, I don't know that you can put a value on playing in March and not only playing but having success and especially beating Duke.
>
> I was in Hawaii a couple of years after that, and I was in a tropical rain forest, and I had on something with "Mercer" on it, and someone asked me, "Are you from Mercer?" I said, "Yes, I am." He said, "I'm from Duke. I can't get away from you guys." So, I'm just like, "Wow, I'm in Hawaii and hearing that?" I don't think you can put a value on that. It's just wide-reaching and widespread for what it has done for us, and it's still to this day doing that. People still bring it up to me, and I don't think you can pay financially for what that win did for our university and our department.

Cole said the feeling and goals around his department have changed, and a lot of that goes back to the win over Duke. Mercer remains an outstanding academic institution, but the coaches and athletes are now competing for conference championships on an annual basis. That wasn't always the case at Mercer.

Entering the 2018–19 school year, Gibson's baseball program had won four regular-season conference titles (2013, 2015, 2016, and 2017) and two conference tournament titles while making three trips to the NCAA Tournament.

Men's soccer head coach Brad Ruzzo's program won the 2014 Southern Conference regular-season titles and the 2016 and 2017 Southern Conference Tournament titles and made trips to the NCAA Tournament in 2016 and 2017. Women's soccer head coach Tony Economopoulos led his team to the 2014 Southern Conference Tournament title and the NCAA Tournament.

Susie Gardner has turned around a struggling women's basketball program that won two games her first season and won the 2018 Southern Conference Tournament title to reach the NCAA Tournament. Gardner's Bears also won the conference regular-season title for the third straight season in 2018. That same spring, the Mercer women's lacrosse team won the inaugural Southern Conference Tournament and advanced to the NCAA Tournament.

With basketball, in particular, Cole said there has been so much recent success that he is having to decide which banners can remain in the Hawkins Arena rafters and which ones might have to come down.

"Our coaches sit in the room now when we're having a meeting and see the success we've had, and they take pride in that," Cole said. "There's not any added pressure from me that, 'You better win,' but they sometimes can put pressure on themselves of, 'I better win.' Winning breeds winning, and our coaches have won a lot the last few years, and we're proud of that."

Hoffman, who once had to tell people he was the head coach of a Division I program, didn't have to sell Mercer quite as hard after that. Mercer, more than ever, sold itself.

It seems to have made a big impact. Even the other day I was at the doctor; I didn't even bring it up, but he said, "That game when you beat Duke, that changed Mercer, that changed Macon." I have heard that several times, and it manifests itself in different ways to different people. I definitely think it was a beginning point for a lot of things that have happened with the university and with us adding other sports and changing leagues. Baseball had been big-time successful already, and Coach Gibson is the best in the nation at what he does, but other than that, we hadn't had a whole lot of success. Now, we have teams winning the league every year, and that's because of the administration and the athletic leadership and Dr. Underwood wanting it to be that way.

His whole vision was for people to know what a good academic institution Mercer was and using athletics as a vehicle to promote the rest of who we were and for us to grow, and that has continued to happen.

It certainly has, and Mercer doesn't want that to change any time soon. Plus, the effects of that day are still visible around campus and still palpable within the university.

"To this day, it comes up. I don't know since then that I have gone on vacation or gone somewhere and people say, 'What do you do?' I say, 'Well, I work at Mercer,' and they respond, 'Well, what do you do at Mercer?' 'Well, I work in marketing and communications, but I also call radio play-by-play.' And I always get, 'Oh, you beat Duke,'" Cameron said. "I figured for the next year we would hear that, but to this day, it's amazing how that plays out. I don't know that it will ever go away, and I hope it doesn't."

Bud Thomas had two points, five assists and three rebounds against Duke. (John Domoney)

12

ALWAYS BEARS

*The 2013–14 Mercer men's basketball team left a legacy
at the university. And those bonds—between the players themselves
and between the players and university—will be there forever.*

The 2013–14 Mercer men's basketball team helped change the school and the school's athletics department. It helped raise the bar, in essence, for everyone involved.

And it will be remembered for just that.

There is a legacy of winning, togetherness, and success that started with the special group of seven seniors. Not only did those players lead that team to unmatched success in Mercer history, but, as some of the players have said, those seniors and the program as a whole did it the right way.

They did it together, focusing on the team first and not the individual pieces, and they did it off the court as well. After all, all seven graduated on time from a strong academic institution.

Those kinds of bonds are difficult to break.

"They'll definitely go down in history at Mercer. I've thought about people going down in the Hall of Fame, but with that group, just about everything they do has to be done as a group," Cole said.

They're that important as a group that everything they should be honored for is together as a group. You just wonder if it will ever happen again—will you have seven guys who are that connected again and were just like a machine with how they played the game?

They knew each other, they knew where they were going to be on the court on both ends without looking because they had been together for so long, and they knew what it took to win games.

The year we beat Duke, everybody graduated on time. That just doesn't happen. It was a special group on the court and off the court, and it still is.

Those seven players meant a lot to the university then, and they will continue to mean a lot to Mercer. Cole points to the A-Sun Tournament championship win as an example of that.

He said he watched the first half of the game, but he couldn't watch the second half. He was too nervous. So, as a former baseball player, he headed over to Florida Gulf Coast's baseball stadium to wait out the outcome of the game.

"I knew about when the game was going to be over, so I kept looking at my watch and checking the time," he said.

So if I saw a flood of people come out, that was good for us. But if I only saw a few people trickle out, that wasn't so good. I walked up to someone and asked what happened, and he said, "Mercer kicked our...butts." I was so nervous I couldn't watch, but I wasn't nervous for me. I was nervous for them. We wanted it for them; everybody did. It was all about them. They had done so much for this university, and all of us, we wanted it for them.

They have just woven themselves into the fabric of Mercer University, and it might be twenty years from now, the ovations and admiration for them will continue. They really were the ones who put Mercer athletics on the map.

Bob Hoffman saw up close just how much those players put into winning that conference title and getting to the NCAA Tournament. He knows what those players—and not just the seniors—mean to Mercer.

"It was an amazing moment and amazing run, an amazing group of men," he said. "It was a culmination to a lot of minutes of hard work by a lot of people to get to that point, and that's special. It means a lot to me, our coaches, and this university."

No matter where they go or where they live—Jake Gollon thinks eventually the seven seniors from that team will start to move closer to one another—they are still bound tightly to Mercer and to one another.

Langston Hall's career has continued in Europe, playing in Italy, Germany, Croatia, and Greece, but he always thinks back on his Mercer playing days and those teammates who became such good friends.

We all started together as freshmen, and we saw where we came from. Our freshman year, we weren't good. Let's just be honest. We thought we could be pretty good, but we had a couple of injuries to the seniors, and the freshmen had to play more and more, and we just weren't good. But every year, we took a step up. Our sophomore year, we ended up going to the CIT and winning the championship, junior year the NIT, and then senior year, finally we go to the NCAA Tournament, so like every year we improved and improved as a team and got better and better. We really deserved it, and the whole time we were together, there was never, "I want to do this" or "I want to average this many points." As long as the team did good, everybody sacrificed, and everything worked out for the best.

People think, "You played in the CIT; what is that?" But we played some good teams and in some tough places, especially the championship game at Utah State. That's the loudest gym I have played in to this day. Not in Raleigh against Duke or at Tennessee or these other places. At one point, it was so loud we couldn't even hear each other in the huddle. They went on a run and had a couple of dunks, and it was so loud, and we were in the huddle. You know, the huddle is pretty close, but Coach Hoffman was talking and we couldn't hear a word. We were just having to read his lips. It was crazy. You think about those moments all the time when you look back on those days.

It's really special just to know that you left your mark as a team and as an individual on a program like that with that much success in a two- or three-year time period. It's crazy to think that in twenty years, we can come back there and can say, "I was on that team that beat Duke," and people are going to remember that.

Gollon's basketball career continued for a few seasons as a college assistant coach, but even after leaving that profession, he knows he will be tied to the game, his teammates, and Mercer for many years to come.

"At this point, there are only a couple of people here and there who live in the same area. I would imagine as the years go on, I think we'll start to see some guys centralize and start to live near each other," he said. He continued,

> If there's a third type of bond, it's not a family, it's not a friend, it's that same sort of shared vision and shared empathy for someone who is chasing the same pursuit as you, and that's a special bond. It's almost more, if it is a family, it's more of a brother or sibling, and I think you tend to see a lot of those guys stay close in each other's lives.
>
> Life is not always as easy as putting a ball through a hoop, but I think you'll see us stay close, and we'll always be tied to Mercer.

Bud Thomas didn't continue his basketball career after leaving Mercer, saying he went back and forth about it and calling it "definitely one of the hardest decisions I ever made to not play in Europe." He still loves the feeling when he returns to Mercer's campus.

> It's a special feeling. All the support from all those people who were just diehard Mercer fans who go to all the games, the away games, to support us. They're still there, and just talking to them, it just all comes back to you. It feels like we were just there getting ready to play Duke. And even walking through the University Center and seeing all the murals and everything and all the banners, it's funny now. I don't want to say it's just now setting in, but when you go back and look at all the stuff we accomplished, in the middle of it, you're not thinking, "We just did this" and "We did that, and no one is ever going to forget it." But looking back and seeing how there are so many banners in that gym, and probably half of them are ours, it's definitely a special feeling for us that we have a strong legacy there and any of us can go back to Mercer and pick right back up with any of those fans or Coach Hoffman as long as he's there. And we'll feel right at home for all the time we spent there.

Daniel Coursey spent two seasons in the G League, the NBA's developmental league, but is now focused on medical school.

"They're my brothers, and we would do anything for each other, and we know any time that we can go back to Mercer, that family is still there, too," he said. "We accomplished a lot, and we worked hard for everything, and it's certainly special to know Mercer will always remember that."

Anthony White played one year in Australia and said he would love to get into coaching and keep his ties to basketball strong. But he knows those connections to his teammates and Mercer won't disappear any time soon.

"One thing I tell my mom and dad all the time is that my son or daughter, when that happens, is going to have a ton of uncles," he said with a laugh.

> They're going to have a ton of uncles to have to deal with and all that good stuff that comes with that. But then again, that's a lot of love to go around.
>
> It's really cool that we made history, not even just at our school, but in the nation. But we don't even talk about it anymore. We're more focused on, "How are you doing?" or "Do you need anything?" If something big happened, like a wedding or Monty getting married and having his son, that's all we talk about now. We don't even talk about beating Duke because honestly I feel like we forget about it sometimes because we are now focused on other things and things that are more important in our lives.

Monty Brown said he hasn't played basketball much since leaving Mercer, even just in pick-up games. It's too hard to match the feeling of playing with his Mercer teammates.

"Being on the team for four years and being around those guys and those coaches, you get so used to that kind of play and doing things the right way and the team mindset," he said. "When you play pick-up ball, everybody is out for themselves, and nobody is talking. It's almost frustrating to say, 'Come on, talk. Let's call out screens and let's talk on defense. Let's spread the floor on offense.' But you forget who you're with, people who have played before and people who have never played before. It's just not the same."

Brown was the first of the seven seniors to get married, and he and his wife, Emerald, were the first to have children, a son named Easton. Brown is looking forward to sharing his memories with his son.

"I definitely started off the trend of getting married and having kids. I wanted to get into it pretty quick," Brown said with a laugh.

> My son isn't old enough to understand it or anything. But I just got goose bumps thinking about, "One day I can show him the rings and tell him the stories of something that's near and dear to my heart." When he's a teenager, he might not listen, but for me, when my dad shared success stories with me of things he was proud of, I know that was cool for him. I can sense those same feelings come on for me as my son gets older day by day.
>
> I've never been one to want notoriety. We liked being noticed as a team, for sure. I liked being noticed. But taking the credit is not what I was looking for. But it's nice because we did it the right way. We didn't recruit dirty or break rules. We didn't take short-cuts. We did it by the book, and we worked our tails off, and that paid off in some very successful stretches down the road. And we can always come back to that.

Kevin Canevari worked at Mercer as a graduate assistant for two years before coaching high school basketball for one season. He returned to Raleigh, the site of Mercer's win and Canevari's best dance moment, as a graduate assistant for NC State in 2017.

"It's great. I love it," he said of his ties to Mercer.

> I have watched almost every game since I graduated. I'll pop open my laptop and watch the game and call Bud and say, "What is he doing? Why is he doing that?" and you want to yell at the laptop at times, and you're pumped about it. It's cool because it's a brotherhood and a family, and seeing how the program works and what Coach Hoffman does, you see how it all ties together. I'm just grateful to have gone through Mercer and had the support of the entire administration and the fans and everyone with the school and what those people mean to me. And especially what my team-mates mean to me.

13

MY THOUGHTS ON THE BEARS

What I remember about the program,
that team, those players, and that season.

When I joined *The Telegraph* sports staff in Macon in 2006 (I took over as sports editor a few months later on January 1, 2007), I was one of those people Bob Hoffman has mentioned who didn't know much about the Mercer basketball program.

I knew what Mercer was. After all, I had lived in the state for several years before that, but I certainly asked, "What's Mercer?" and "Wait, Mercer is a Division I program?"

I tend to think I know just a *little bit* about sports after being in sports journalism since I was eighteen years old. Still, I had very little knowledge about Mercer or its basketball program.

Even after I got to Macon, there just wasn't a lot of interest in Mercer basketball, and there was zero buzz. That's understandable. Mercer is a small private school and hadn't really done much, that I could tell anyway, to be a bigger part of the community.

Plus, the basketball program just wasn't very good.

That all changed quickly once Hoffman took over. It was easy to see a change in the energy surrounding the program. There was an excitement Coach Hoffman brought to Mercer and to Macon, and his passion for the game rubbed off on anyone who was around him for any amount of time.

He knew he had to sell his program, and he set out to do just that as soon as he got to Mercer. You know, the old "hit the ground running" philosophy; that was Hoffman.

I had never heard of Bob Hoffman, to be honest, before he was in the mix to get the job, but my first interaction with him erased any doubts about what he brought to Mercer and Macon as a whole. I was coaching my sons, Ben and Matt, in youth basketball, along with a good friend, Jarome Gautreaux, who is a Mercer graduate. Before we started the season, all the coaches took part in a coach's clinic with Hoffman, and it was definitely a memorable day.

It was a random Saturday morning with a bunch of people who didn't know much about coaching basketball—or maybe I should just speak for myself—and Hoffman could have been anywhere else but there: you know, working on building his new program, looking for players, working with the ones he already had. But he saw this as a perfect chance to help build his program. He got out in the community and shared his vision and passion for what he wanted to accomplish with Mercer basketball.

And he shared his passion for the game, in general, and doing things the right way, what coaching should be. Not screaming and yelling and doing everything to win a game (even crossing the line, which many coaches do a lot). No, coaching is teaching and molding young people to help them grow through their lives, and Hoffman is terrific at all of aspects of it.

I left the gym that morning and said to Jarome something to the effect of, "Man, that guy is impressive." I knew that day that Mercer was going to change, the basketball program, at least. I certainly didn't foresee everything else that would come with that.

But, again, it was a long road to get there.

There was a lot of excitement when the A-Sun announced it would play its men's and women's basketball tournaments at Mercer for two years. It went so well that the conference added two more years.

That was an exciting time to be a sports writer and a sports fan in Macon, as it was easy to see something special building with Hoffman's program. There isn't much in sports that can equal a day of tournament basketball, and there were a lot of long days and hard work that went into our coverage of that tournament from my terrific staff at *The Telegraph*.

There were a couple of close calls, too, as Mercer just couldn't get over the hump to win the conference tournament even with it being played on its own campus. The two Florida Gulf Coast losses—in the semifinals in 2011–12 and in the championship game in 2012–13—were excruciating. I'm not sure I have heard that arena as loud before or since as the start of the semifinal game in 2011–12. Sitting on press row, it was hard to think because it was so loud, and I remember just taking in the huge crowd there for the game (remember, it wasn't like that before Hoffman took over) and looking up to see my wife, Laura, and my sons sitting in the stands.

On the other end of the spectrum, it was almost dead silent after the game as a small contingent of Florida Gulf Coast fans celebrated their team's upset win.

The scene was similar the next year. Loud before the game with a lot of anticipation, but things changed in the end as the Eagles took control and pulled away for the win.

I vividly remember interviewing Langston Hall after the game and thinking he deserved better, his teammates deserved better, Hoffman deserved better. Yes, Hall was disappointed, but he kept his head up and stayed determined, and he wasn't the only one. When the next season came around, it was easy to see that Hall and his teammates still had that determination and had big things on their minds for that season.

Michael A. Lough, who handled most of the coverage for the team for *The Telegraph* back then, even told me before the season that he thought that it would be the Bears' year, that they would finally get it done. I believed him, but I also knew they would have to finally get past their nemesis—Florida Gulf Coast—to get it done.

They did just that, and that was a special group in 2013–14.

Jake Gollon was a terrific player, a fighter, a competitor who would do everything it took to win. Hall, I think, was the key to it all. I do remember watching him as a freshman and wondering why he wasn't at Georgia or Georgia Tech, and he only got better as his career went along. He was just so clutch that you thought he was always going to come up with the winning play every time, and he was as smooth, calm, cool, and collected as any point guard I've ever seen play in person.

Daniel Coursey and Monty Brown (and T. J. Hallice, too) combined to be a force on the inside. Bud Thomas was ridiculously fun to watch; a shooter who can also defend like that is rare. White was deadly and confident, and he hit a *lot* of big shots in his two seasons with the program. Kevin Canevari competed every minute he was on the floor. Like Hoffman said, if Canevari played ten minutes, he gave the Bears his best ten minutes. Ike Nwamu and Darious Moten gave the team an athletic component that was huge against power conference teams, and they both made big plays that championship season. I remember seeing Nwamu in the preseason dunking left and right and thinking, "My goodness. That's new." I may have added some colorful language in there, too.

That season was special from the start, and right before the seniors' final home game, Lough sat down with them and talked about their careers—or let them talk—as he came up with a terrific piece on the seven of them going back and forth about each other, their time at Mercer, what it meant to play for Hoffman, etc.

As I read it, I thought, "They're good. This group is ready to go." I was thinking just about the A-Sun Tournament and finally getting past Florida Gulf Coast. I had no idea what would come after that. No one could see that coming, right? Well, maybe Hoffman did.

But that long-needed win over Florida Gulf Coast was special. Sure, sports writers are supposed to stay neutral and to not cheer for the teams we cover, but it's hard to not want good things to happen to good people. And Bob Hoffman and his players were (and are) good people.

Next came the wacky, wild day of the NCAA Tournament selection show, and the arena erupted when "Mercer" popped up on the screen next to "Duke." That was one of those moments covering sports I'll never forget. But *Duke*? *Really*?

Lough headed to Raleigh, and thinking back on it, it would have been great to go with him or at least send another staff writer with him. But newspaper budgets can be, well, tight, silly, and shortsighted. It certainly was that day. We could have sent four or five people and still would have needed to get Lough more help with what he was about to experience. But he handled it like a pro and churned out some really good copy those crazy few days.

I watched the game with my wife, Laura, Gautreaux, his wife, Mitzi, and some other friends at a restaurant right across the street from *The Telegraph* office in Mercer Village. Sitting there watching the game, I was thinking, "Just keep it close. That would be big." But to see that team persevere and overcome Duke in the middle of all those Mercer fans was exciting, exhilarating, and thrilling, whatever adjective you want to attach to it.

And that was just probably about 10 percent of what the folks in Raleigh were feeling.

Then Canevari started dancing. Wait. What? What in the world is going on? And then all hell broke loose.

I rushed back over to the office, and we got to work. But it certainly was a fun (but long) day of work. When you love what you're doing, it's not really work, right? And we loved putting out the paper that day.

We went back and forth on headlines for the next day's paper. I wanted to go with "Bear-deviled" but got shot down as a pitch for the front page of the newspaper. That section went with "Lord have Mercer," which is a good one, for sure, as we tried to capture the moment that the entire college basketball world just saw and tried to make sense of.

I will say, however, that it was our sports front with "Bear-deviled" and not the front page with "Lord have Mercer" that ESPN decided to display behind its *SportsCenter* anchors. As I said that day, "I'll take it."

That was a wild, special, crazy couple of days. Sure, Mercer's season came to an end that Sunday with the loss to Tennessee, but that couldn't take anything away from what Hoffman, his staff, and those players accomplished.

They lifted up Mercer University and Macon, Georgia, too, and it was fun to go along for the ride.

SPECIAL THANKS
TO MY VALUABLE SOURCES:

Justin Baxley | Monty Brown | Rick Cameron

Kevin Canevari | Jim Cole | Daniel Coursey

Jake Gollon | Langston Hall | T. J. Hallice

Jane Heeter | Bob Hoffman | Kelli Hoffman

Carrie Ingoldsby | Thomas Norton | Doug Pearson

Cindy Strowbridge | Bud Thomas | Jeremy Timmerman

Bill Underwood | Anthony White